T0179349

JavaScript for Data Science

Chapman & Hall/CRC Data Science Series

About the Series

Reflecting the interdisciplinary nature of the field, this new book series brings together researchers, practitioners, and instructors from statistics, computer science, machine learning, and analytics. The series will publish cutting-edge research, industry applications, and textbooks in data science.

Features:

- Presents the latest research and applications in the field, including new statistical and computational techniques
- Covers a broad range of interdisciplinary topics
- Provides guidance on the use of software for data science, including R, Python, and Julia
- Includes both introductory and advanced material for students and professionals
- Presents concepts while assuming minimal theoretical background

The scope of the series is broad, including titles in machine learning, pattern recognition, predictive analytics, business analytics, visualization, programming, software, learning analytics, data collection and wrangling, interactive graphics, reproducible research, and more. The inclusion of examples, applications, and code implementation is essential.

JavaScript for Data Science
Maya Gans, Toby Hodges, Greg Wilson

Basketball Data Science: With Applications in R
Paola Zuccolotto, Marica Manisera

Cybersecurity Analytics
Rakesh M. Verma, David J. Marchette

Introduction to Data Science: Data Analysis and Prediction Algorithms with R
Rafael A. Irizarry

Feature Engineering and Selection: A Practical Approach for Predictive Models
Max Kuhn, Kjell Johnson

Probability and Statistics for Data Science: Math + R + Data
Norman Matloff

JavaScript for Data Science

Maya Gans
Toby Hodges
Greg Wilson

CRC Press
Taylor & Francis Group
Boca Raton London New York

CRC Press is an imprint of the
Taylor & Francis Group, an **informa** business

A CHAPMAN & HALL BOOK

CRC Press
Taylor & Francis Group
6000 Broken Sound Parkway NW, Suite 300
Boca Raton, FL 33487-2742

Printed on acid-free paper

International Standard Book Number-13: 978-0-367-42248-6 (Paperback)
International Standard Book Number-13: 978-0-367-42652-1 (Hardback)

Visit the Taylor & Francis Web site at
http://www.taylorandfrancis.com

and the CRC Press Web site at
http://www.crcpress.com

Dedication

———————

For Jordan
who taught me failures pave the way to success.
— Maya

For Oskar.
— Toby

For Kara, Claudia, Erin, Gabriela, Hannah, Laura, and Julia.
— Greg

All royalties from the sale of this book are being donated to R-Ladies,
a worldwide organization whose mission is
to promote gender diversity in the R community.

Contents

1 Introduction

David Beazley[1] thought that "JavaScript *versus* Data Science" would be a better title for this book. While that one word sums up how many people view the language, we hope we can convince you that modern JavaScript is usable as well as useful. Scientists and engineers are who we were thinking of when we wrote this book but we hope that these lessons will also help librarians, digital humanists, and everyone else who uses computing in their research.

We will cover:

· Core features of modern JavaScript
· Programming with callbacks and promises
· Creating objects and classes
· Writing HTML and CSS
· Creating interactive pages with React
· Building data services
· Testing
· Data visualization
· Combining everything to create a three-tier web application

Unlike most introductions to JavaScript, these lessons present an even mix of browser programming and server programming. We give each topic only shallow coverage; if you want to know more, there are many other free tutorials you can dive into once you've mastered the basics, some of which are both up-to-date and well designed.

1.1 WHO YOU ARE

Every lesson should aim to meet the needs of specific learners[2] **[Wils2019]**. The three people described below define the intended audience for this one.

Bhadra received a BSc in microbiology five years ago, and has worked since then for a biotech firm with labs in four countries. She did a statistics class using R as an undergrad, then learned some more R and some Unix shell scripting in a Software Carpentry[3] workshop, but has no other training as a programmer. Bhadra's team is developing tools to detect structural similarities between proteins. They would like to build a browser interface to their tools so that people can test different algorithms on various datasets. This book will show Bhadra how to build, test, and deploy that interface.

---

[1] https://www.dabeaz.com/

[2] http://teachtogether.tech/en/process/

[3] http://software-carpentry.org/

Efraim did fieldwork for the Ministry of Natural Resources for thirty-one years. He learned Visual Basic so that he could write Excel macros, then mastered C in order to maintain the control software for some second-hand remote sensing equipment. Efraim recently retired, and is now an active member of several citizen science projects. This book will show him how to create a service to share those projects' data with the world, and how to build a web-based administrative interface for it.

Sumi is completing a PhD in 19th Century history. As part of her research, she is transcribing and cataloging the records of several dozen Japanese-American midwives. She has been creating and customizing WordPress sites for several years, and has picked up bits and pieces of JavaScript while doing so. Sumi is about to start looking for a job, and wants to create an interactive website to showcase her research. This book will fill in some of the gaps in her knowledge and show her how to take advantage of JavaScript's more modern features.

These prototypical users:

- can write two-page programs that use lists, loops, conditionals, and functions,
- can run commands in the Unix shell to navigate the filesystem and create and delete directories and files, and
- have reliable access to the Internet.

1.2 WHO WE ARE

Maya Gans is a freelance data scientist and front-end developer by way of quantitative biology. She has 4 years of experience programming in R, and her passion for data visualization brought her to the weird world of JavaScript. When she isn't debugging or blogging[4] about code, she's somewhere remote climbing large mountains. She dedicates this book to her fellow self-taught programmers who were told they weren't good enough but are too driven and excited to care.

Toby Hodges[5] is a bioinformatician turned community coordinator, working on the Bio-IT Project[6] at EMBL[7]. He teaches a lot of courses in computing, organizes a lot of community-building events, listens to a lot of punk rock, and occasionally still finds time to write code and ride his bike. Toby would like to thank his wife for her support and patience while he swore about how annoying JavaScript is to debug.

Greg Wilson[8] has worked for 35 years in both industry and academia, and is the author or editor of several books on computing and two for children. He co-founded Software Carpentry[9], a non-profit organization that teaches basic computing skills

---

[4]https://maya.rbind.io/

[5]https://tbyhdgs.info/

[6]https://bio-it.embl.de

[7]https://www.embl.de

[8]http://third-bit.com/

[9]http://carpentries.org

to researchers, and is now part of the education team at RStudio[10]. Greg would like to thank everyone at Rangle[11] who was so patient with him when he was learning JavaScript.

1.3 SETTING UP

You can find the examples for each chapter in the src directory in our GitHub repository[12]. Each sub-folder contains the code and data needed to follow along with the text.

The exercises at the end of each chapter include new information that you will need later in the book, and are therefore not optional. You can do the first few online, using a service like RunKit[13], which gives you an interactive JavaScript playground in your browser. For larger things, and for chapters starting with the one on creating dynamic web pages (Chapter 7), you should download and install[14] the latest Long-term Support (LTS) versions of Node and NPM.

Node is an open source implementation of JavaScript that includes a command-line interpreter like those for languages such as Python and R. The command node on its own starts a **read-evaluate-print loop** (REPL) that executes commands as they are typed in and displays their output. The command node filename.js reads and runs the commands in filename.js; we will see in Chapter 6 how to run JavaScript in a browser.

npm is the Node **Package Manager**, a command-line tool for finding, installing, updating, building, and executing JavaScript libraries. The command npm install --global library-name (without a .js extension) installs a library **globally** so that all projects can use it, while npm install --save library-name installs the library **locally** (i.e., in the current project folder). Local installation is usually a better idea, since it isolates projects from one another.

1.4 CONTRIBUTING

Contributions of all kinds are welcome, from errata and minor improvements to entirely new sections and chapters: please submit an issue or pull request to our GitHub repository[15]. Everyone whose work is incorporated will be acknowledged; please note that all contributors are required to abide by our Code of Conduct (Appendix B). Please note that we use Simplified English rather than Traditional English,

---

[10]http://rstudio.com

[11]https://rangle.io/

[12]https://github.com/software-tools-in-javascript/js4ds

[13]https://runkit.com/

[14]https://nodejs.org/en/download/

[15]https://github.com/software-tools-in-javascript/js4ds/

i.e., American rather than British spelling and grammar. We encourage translations; if you would like to take this on, please email us[16].

If you wish to report errata or suggest improvements to wording, please include the chapter name in the first line of the body of your report (e.g., `Testing Data Analysis`).

1.4.1 ACKNOWLEDGMENTS

We are grateful as always to Shashi Kumar for help with the LaTeX. We are also grateful for fixes from:

- Stephan Druskat[17]
- Chiranjeev Gupta[18]
- Eric Leung[19]
- Peter Munro[20]
- Leonardo Uieda[21]

1.5 EXERCISES

SETTING UP

Install Node[22] on your computer, then run the commands `node --version` and npm `--version` to see which versions you have.

KEY POINTS

- Modern JavaScript is a good tool for building desktop and web-based applications.
- This course is for people who know what loops and functions are, but have never used JavaScript or built web applications.
- Node is a command-line interpreter for JavaScript, which can be used interactively or to run scripts in files.
- NPM is the Node Package Manager, which can be used to find, install, update, build, and execute JavaScript libraries.

---

[16] gvwilson@third-bit.com

[17] https://github.com/sdruskat

[18] https://github.com/cRAN-cg

[19] https://erictleung.com/

[20] https://github.com/pdm55

[21] http://www.leouieda.com/

[22] https://nodejs.org/en/download/

2 Basic Features

This lesson introduces the core features of JavaScript, including how to run programs, the language's basic data types, arrays and objects, loops, conditionals, functions, and modules. All of these concepts should be familiar if you have programmed before.

2.1 HELLO, WORLD

Use your favorite text editor to put the following line in a file called `hello.js`:

```
console.log('hello, world')
```

`console` is a built-in **module** that provides basic printing services (among other things). As in many languages, we use the **dotted notation** `X.Y` to get part `Y` of thing `X`—in this case, to get `console`'s `log` function. **Character strings** like `'hello, world'` can be written with either single quotes or double quotes, so long as the quotation marks match, and semi-colons at the ends of statements are now (mostly) optional.

To run a program, type `node program_name.js` at the command line. (We will preface shell commands with $ to make them easier to spot.)

```
$ node src/basics/hello.js

hello, world
```

2.2 BASIC DATA TYPES

JavaScript has the usual datatypes, though unlike C, Python, and many other languages, there is no separate type for integers: it stores all numbers as 64-bit floating-point values, which is accurate up to about 15 decimal digits. We can check this using `typeof`, which returns a string. (Note: `typeof` is an operator, *not* a function: we apply it to something by typing a space followed by the name of the thing we'd like to check the type of, e.g., `typeof dress` as opposed to `typeof(dress)`.) We use it alongside `const` below, which itself is helpful when we want to give a name to a **constant** value:

```
const aNumber = 123.45
console.log('the type of', aNumber, 'is', typeof aNumber)

the type of 123.45 is number

const anInteger = 123
console.log('the type of', anInteger, 'is', typeof anInteger)
```

5

```
the type of 123 is number
```

We have already met strings, which may contain any **Unicode** character:

```
const aString = 'some text'
console.log('the type of', aString, 'is', typeof aString)
```

```
the type of some text is string
```

Functions are also a type of data, a fact whose implications we will explore in Chapter 3:

```
console.log('the type of', console.log, 'is', typeof console.log)
```

```
the type of function () { [native code] } is function
```

Rather than showing the other basic types one by one, we will put three values in a list and loop over it:

```
const otherValues = [true, undefined, null]
for (let value of otherValues) {
  console.log('the type of', value, 'is', typeof value)
}
```

```
the type of true is boolean
the type of undefined is undefined
the type of null is object
```

As the example above shows, we create an array of values to loop through called `otherValues`. We initiate our loop with the word `for`. Within the parentheses, `let` creates a variable called `value` to iterate over each element within `otherValues`, and `value` is the changing array value of `otherValues`. Finally, within the curly braces we perform our desired operation on every value.

Note that we use `let` rather than the older `var` and `of` rather than `in`: the latter returns the indexes of the collection (e.g., 0, 1, 2), which has some traps for the unwary (Appendix G.2). Note also that indexing starts from 0 rather than 1, and that indentation is optional and for readability purposes only. This may be different from the language that you're used to.

Constants versus Variables
You should make things constants unless they really need to be variables because it's easier for both people and computers to keep track of things that are defined once and never change.

After all this, the types themselves are somewhat anticlimactic. JavaScript's **boolean** type can be either `true` or `false`, though we will see below that other things can be treated as Booleans. `undefined` means "hasn't been given a value", while `null` means "has a value, which is nothing".

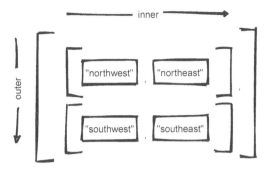

Figure 2.1: Nested Loop Traversal

2.3 CONTROL FLOW

We have already seen for loops and flat arrays, so let's have a look at nested arrays and conditionals. We start with arrays that contain other arrays, which are usually processed by **nested loops**:

```
const nested = [['northwest', 'northeast'],
                ['southwest', 'southeast']]
for (let outer of nested) {
  for (let inner of outer) {
    console.log(inner)
  }
}

northwest
northeast
southwest
southeast
```

The **inner loop** runs a complete cycle of iterations for each iteration of the **outer loop**. Each value assigned to the variable outer is a pair, so each value assigned to inner is one of the two strings from that pair (Figure 2.1).

A JavaScript program can also make choices: it executes the **body** of an if statement if and only if the **condition** is true. Each if can have an else, whose body is only executed if the condition *isn't* true:

```
const values = [0, 1, '', 'text', undefined, null, [], [2, 3]]
for (let element of values) {
  if (element) {
    console.log(element, 'of type', typeof element, 'is truthy')
  } else {
    console.log(element, 'of type', typeof element, 'is falsy')
  }
}

0 of type number is falsy
1 of type number is truthy
```

```
 of type string is falsy
text of type string is truthy
undefined of type undefined is falsy
null of type object is falsy
 of type object is truthy
2,3 of type object is truthy
```

This example shows that arrays are **heterogeneous**, i.e., that they can contain values of many different types. It also shows that JavaScript has some rather odd ideas about the nature of truth. 0 is **falsy**, while all other numbers are **truthy**; similarly, the empty string is falsy and all other strings are truthy. undefined and null are both falsy, as most programmers would expect.

But as the last two lines of output show, an empty array is truthy, which is different from its treatment in most programming languages. The argument made by JavaScript's advocates is that an empty array is there, it just happens to be empty, but this behavior is still a common cause of bugs. When testing an array, check that Array.length is zero. (Note that this is a **property**, not a **method**, i.e., it should be treated as a variable, not called like a function.)

Safety Tip
Always use === (triple equals) and !== when testing for equality and inequality in JavaScript. == and != do type conversion, which can produce some ugly surprises (Section G.1).

2.4 FORMATTING STRINGS

Rather than printing multiple strings and expressions, we can **interpolate** values into a back-quoted string. (We have to use back quotes because this feature was added to JavaScript long after the language was first created.) As the example below shows, the value to be interpolated is put in ${...}, and can be any valid JavaScript expression, including a function or method call.

```
for (let color of ['red', 'green', 'blue']) {
  const message = `color is ${color}`
  console.log(message, `and capitalized is ${color.toUpperCase()}`)
}

color is red and capitalized is RED
color is green and capitalized is GREEN
color is blue and capitalized is BLUE
```

This allows us to succinctly add variables to a string instead of:

```
const message = "color is" + color + "and capitalized is " + color.toUpperCase()
```

2.5 OBJECTS

An **object** in JavaScript is a collection of key-value pairs, and is equivalent in simple cases to what Python would call a dictionary. It's common to visualize an object as a

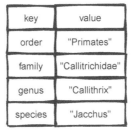

key	value
order	"Primates"
family	"Callitrichidae"
genus	"Callithrix"
species	"Jacchus"

Figure 2.2: Objects in Memory

two-column table with the keys in one column and the values in another (Figure 2.2). The keys must be strings; the values can be anything. We can create an object by putting key-value pairs in curly brackets; there must be a colon between the key and the value, and pairs must be separated by commas like the elements of arrays:

```
const creature = {
  'order': 'Primates',
  'family': 'Callitrichidae',
  'genus': 'Callithrix',
  'species': 'Jacchus'
}

console.log(`creature is ${creature}`)
console.log(`creature.genus is ${creature.genus}`)
for (let key in creature) {
  console.log(`creature[${key}] is ${creature[key]}`)
}


creature is [object Object]
creature.genus is Callithrix
creature[order] is Primates
creature[family] is Callitrichidae
creature[genus] is Callithrix
creature[species] is Jacchus
```

The type of an object is always `object`. We can get the value associated with a key using `object[key]`, but if the key has a simple name, we can use `object.key` instead. Note that the square bracket form can be used with variables for keys, but the dotted notation cannot: i.e., `creature.genus` is the same as `creature['genus']`, but the assignment `g = 'genus'` followed by `creature.g` does not work.

Because string keys are so common, and because programmers use simple names so often, JavaScript allows us to create objects without quoting the names of the keys:

```
const creature = {
  order: 'Primates',
  family: 'Callitrichidae',
```

```
  genus: 'Callithrix',
  species: 'Jacchus'
}
```

[object Object] is not particularly useful output when we want to see
what an object contains. To get a more helpful string representation, use
JSON.stringify(object):

```
console.log(JSON.stringify(creature))
```

```
{"order":"Primates","family":"Callitrichidae",
 "genus":"Callithrix","species":"Jacchus"}
```

Here, "JSON" stands for "JavaScript Object Notation"; we will learn more about it
in Chapter 11.

2.6 FUNCTIONS

Functions make it possible for mere mortals to understand programs by allowing us
to think about them one piece at a time. Here is a function that finds the lowest and
highest values in an array:

```
function limits (values) {
  if (!values.length) {
    return [undefined, undefined]
  }
  let low = values[0]
  let high = values[0]
  for (let v of values) {
    if (v < low) low = v
    if (v > high) high = v
  }
  return [low, high]
}
```

Its definition consists of the keyword function, its name, a parenthesized list of
parameters (which might be empty), and its body.

The body of the function begins with a test of the thing, referred to inside
the function as values, provided as an **argument** to the function. If values
has no length—i.e., it does not consist of multiple entries—the function returns
[undefined,undefined]. (We will address the rationale behind this behavior in
the exercises.)

```
  if (!values.length) {
    return [undefined, undefined]
  }
```

If that initial check finds that values does have a length—i.e., !values.length
returns false—the rest of the function is run. This involves first initializing two
variables, low and high, with their values set as equal to the first item in values.

```
let low = values[0]
let high = values[0]
```

In the next stage of the function, all of the values are iterated over and `low` and `high` are assigned a new value, equal to that of the next item, if that value is lower than `low` or higher than `high` respectively.

```
for (let v of values) {
  if (v < low) low = v
  if (v > high) high = v
}
```

Once all of the items in `values` have been examined, the values of `low` and `high` are the minimum and maximum of `values`. These are returned as a pair inside an array.

```
return [low, high]
```

Note that we can use `return` to explicitly return a value at any time; if nothing is returned, the function's result is `undefined`.

One oddity of JavaScript is that almost anything can be compared to almost anything else. Here are a few tests that demonstrate this:

```
const allTests = [
  [],
  [9],
  [3, 30, 300],
  ['apple', 'Grapefruit', 'banana'],
  [3, 'apple', ['sub-array']]
]
for (let test of allTests) {
  console.log(`limits of ${test} are ${limits(test)}`)
}
```

```
limits of  are ,
limits of 9 are 9,9
limits of 3,30,300 are 3,300
limits of apple,Grapefruit,banana are Grapefruit,banana
limits of 3,apple,sub-array are 3,3
```

Programmers generally don't write functions this way any longer, since it interacts in odd ways with other features of the language; Section G.3 explains why and how in more detail. Instead, most programmers now write **fat arrow functions** consisting of a parameter list, the => symbol, and a body. Fat arrow functions don't have names, so the function must be assigned that to a constant or variable for later use:

```
const limits = (values) => {
  if (!values.length) {
    return [undefined, undefined]
  }
```

```
let low = values[0]
let high = values[0]
for (let v of values) {
  if (v < low) low = v
  if (v > high) high = v
}
return [low, high]
}
```

No matter how functions are defined, each one is a **scope**, which means its parameters and any variables created inside it are **local** to the function. We will discuss scope in more detail in Chapter 3.

> ### *Stuck in the Past*
> *Why did JavaScript introduce another syntax rather than fixing the behavior of those defined with* function*? The twin answers are that changes would break legacy programs that rely on the old behavior, and that the language's developers wanted to make it really easy to define little functions. Here and elsewhere, we will see how a language's history and use shape its evolution.*

2.7 MODULES

As our programs grow larger, we will want to put code in multiple files. The unavoidable bad news is that JavaScript has several module systems: Node still uses one called CommonJS, but is converting to the modern standard called ES6, so what we use on the command line is different from what we use in the browser (for now).

> ### *Ee Ess*
> *JavaScript's official name is ECMAScript, though only people who use the word "datum" in everyday conversation ever call it that. Successive versions of the language are therefore known as ES5, ES6, and so on, except when they're referred to as (for example) ES2018.*

Since we're going to build command-line programs before doing anything in the browser, we will introduce Node's module system first (Figure 2.3). We start by putting this code in a file called utilities.js:

```
DEFAULT_BOUND = 3

const clip = (values, bound = DEFAULT_BOUND) => {
  let result = []
  for (let v of values) {
    if (v <= bound) {
      result.push(v)
    }
  }
  return result
}
```

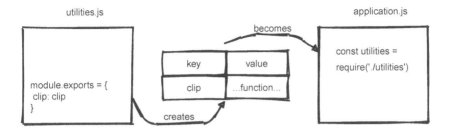

Figure 2.3: How Require Works

```
module.exports = {
  clip: clip
}
```

The function definition is straightforward; as you may have guessed, bound = DEFAULT_BOUND sets a default value for that parameter so that clip can be called with just an array. You may also have guessed that Array.push appends a value to the end of an array; if you didn't, well, now you know.

What's more important is assigning an object to module.exports. Only those things named in this object are visible to the outside world, so DEFAULT_BOUND won't be. Remember, keys that are simple names don't have to be quoted, so clip: clip means "associate a reference to the function clip with the string key "clip".

To use our newly-defined module we must require it. For example, we can put this in application.js:

```
const utilities = require('./utilities')

const data = [-1, 5, 3, 0, 10]
console.log(`clip(${data}) -> ${utilities.clip(data)}`)
console.log(`clip(${data}, 5) -> ${utilities.clip(data, 5)}`)

clip(-1,5,3,0,10) -> -1,3,0
clip(-1,5,3,0,10, 5) -> -1,5,3,0
```

require returns the object that was assigned to module.exports, so if we have assigned its result to a variable called utilities, we must then call our function as utilities.clip. We use a relative path starting with ./ or ../ to import local files; paths that start with names are taken from installed Node libraries.

2.8 EXERCISES

TYPEOF

What kind of thing is typeof? Is it an expression? A function? Something else? (You might notice that typeof typeof is syntactically invalid. In such circumstances, an Internet search engine is your friend, as is the Mozilla Developer Network[1] JavaScript reference.

FILL IN THE BLANKS

Answer these questions about the program below:

1. What does `Array.push` do?
2. How does a `while` loop work?
3. What does `+=` do?
4. What does `Array.reverse` do, and what does it return?

```
let current = 0
let table = []
while (current < 5) {
  const entry = `square of ${current} is ${current * current}`
  table.push(entry)
  current += 1
}
table.reverse()
for (let line of table) {
  console.log(line)
}

square of 4 is 16
square of 3 is 9
square of 2 is 4
square of 1 is 1
square of 0 is 0
```

WHAT IS TRUTH?

Write a function called `isTruthy` that returns `true` for everything that JavaScript considers truthy, and `false` for everything it considers falsy *except* empty arrays: `isTruthy` should return `false` for those.

THE SHAPE OF THINGS TO COME

We wrote the example function, `limits`, above to return `[undefined,undefined]` if a variable with no length is fed into it. What is the advantage of doing this as opposed to returning `undefined` only?

COMBINING DIFFERENT TYPES

What does `NaN` represent? What output would you expect from the code below? Try running it and see whether the results match your expectations. What are the implications of this behavior when working with real-world data?

[1] https://developer.mozilla.org/en-US/docs/Web/JavaScript/Reference

```
const first = [3, 7, 8, 9, 1]
console.log(`aggregating ${first}`)
let total = 0
for (let d of first) {
  total += d
}
console.log(total)

const second = [0, 3, -1, NaN, 8]
console.log(`aggregating ${second}`)
total = 0
for (let d of second) {
  total += d
}
console.log(total)
```

WHAT DOES THIS DO?

Explain what is happening in the assignment statement that creates the constant creature.

```
const genus = 'Callithrix'
const species = 'Jacchus'
const creature = {genus, species}
console.log(creature)

{ genus: 'Callithrix', species: 'Jacchus' }
```

DESTRUCTURING ASSIGNMENT

When this short program runs:

```
const creature = {
  genus: 'Callithrix',
  species: 'Jacchus'
}
const {genus, species} = creature
console.log(`genus is ${genus}`)
console.log(`species is ${species}`)
```

it produces the output:

```
genus is Callithrix
species is Jacchus
```

but when this program runs:

```
const creature = {
  first: 'Callithrix',
  second: 'Jacchus'
}
const {genus, species} = creature
console.log(`genus is ${genus}`)
console.log(`species is ${species}`)
```

it produces:

```
genus is undefined
species is undefined
```

1. What is the difference between these two programs?
2. How does **destructuring assignment** work in general?
3. How can we use this technique to rewrite the `require` statement in
   `src/basics/import.js` so that `clip` can be called directly as `clip(...)`
   rather than as `utilities.clip(...)`?

RETURN TO ME, FOR MY HEART WANTS YOU ONLY

What output would you see in the console if you ran this code?

```
const verbose_sum = (first, second) => {
  console.log(`Going to add ${first} to ${second}`)
  let total = first + second
  return total
  console.log(`Finished summing`)
}

var result = verbose_sum(3, 6)
console.log(result)
```

1. Going to add ${first} to ${second}
   9
2. Going to add 3 to 6
   9
   Finished summing
3. Going to add 3 to 6
   9
4. Going to add 3 to 6
   36

KEY POINTS

- Use `console.log` to print messages.
- Use dotted notation `X.Y` to get part `Y` of object `X`.
- Basic data types are Booleans, numbers, and character strings.
- Arrays store multiple values in order.
- The special values `null` and `undefined` mean 'no value' and 'does not exist'.
- Define constants with `const` and variables with `let`.
- `typeof` returns the type of a value.
- `for (let variable of collection) {...}` iterates through the values in
  an array.
- `if (condition) {...} else {...}` conditionally executes some code.

- `false`, 0, the empty string, `null`, and `undefined` are false; everything else is true.
- Use back quotes and `${...}` to interpolate values into strings.
- An object is a collection of name/value pairs written in `{...}`.
- `object[key]` or `object.key` gets a value from an object.
- Functions are objects that can be assigned to variables, stored in lists, etc.
- `function name(...parameters...) {...body...}` is the old way to define a function.
- `name = (...parameters...) => {...body...}` is the new way to define a function.
- Use `return` inside a function body to return a value at any point.
- Use modules to divide code between multiple files for re-use.
- Assign to `module.exports` to specify what a module exports.
- `require(...path...)` imports a module.
- Paths beginning with '.' or '/' are imported locally, but paths without '.' or '/' look in the library.

3 Callbacks

JavaScript relies heavily on **callback functions**: Instead of a function giving us a result immediately, we give it another function that tells it what to do next. Many other languages use them as well, but JavaScript is often the first place that programmers with data science backgrounds encounter them. In order to understand how they work and how to use them, we must first understand what actually happens when functions are defined and called.

3.1 THE CALL STACK

When JavaScript **parses** the expression `let name = "text"`, it allocates a block of memory big enough for four characters and stores a reference to that block of characters in the variable `name`. We can show this by drawing a **memory diagram** like the one in Figure 3.1.

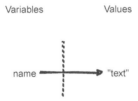

Figure 3.1: Name and Value

When we write:

```
oneMore = (x) => {
  return x + 1
}
```

JavaScript allocates a block of memory big enough to store several instructions, translates the text of the function into instructions, and stores a reference to those instructions in the variable `oneMore` (Figure 3.2).

The only difference between these two cases is what's on the other end of the reference: four characters or a bunch of instructions that add one to a number. This means that we can assign the function to another variable, just as we would assign a number:

```
// assign the function oneMore to the variable anotherName
const anotherName = oneMore

// instead of calling the function oneMore we can call the function anotherName
console.log(anotherName(5))
```

6

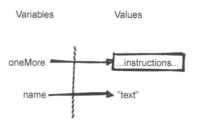

Figure 3.2: Functions in Memory

Doing this does *not* call the function: as Figure 3.3 shows, it creates a second name, or **alias**, that refers to the same block of instructions.

As explained in Chapter 2, when JavaScript calls a function it assigns the arguments in the call to the function's parameters. In order for this to be safe, we need to ensure that there are no **name collisions**, i.e., that if there is a variable called something and one of the function's parameters is also called something, the function will use the right one. The way every modern language implements this is to use a **call stack**. Instead of putting all our variables in one big table, we have one table for global variables and one extra table for each function call. This means that if we assign 100 to x, call oneMore(2 * x + 1), and look at memory in the middle of that call, we will see what's in Figure 3.4.

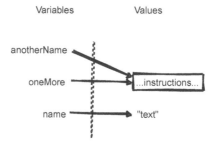

Figure 3.3: Aliasing a Function

3.2 FUNCTIONS OF FUNCTIONS

The call stack allows us to write and call functions without worrying about whether we're accidentally going to refer to the wrong variable. And since functions are just another kind of data, we can pass one function into another. For example, we can write a function called doTwice that calls some other function two times:

```
const doTwice = (action) => {
  action()
```

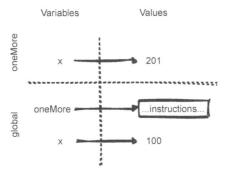

Figure 3.4: The Call Stack

```
    action()
}

const hello = () => {
  console.log('hello')
}

doTwice(hello)

hello
hello
```

Again, this is clearer when we look at the state of memory while doTwice is running (Figure 3.5).

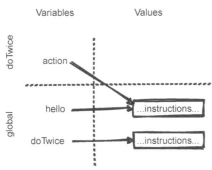

Figure 3.5: Functions of Functions

This becomes more useful when the function or functions passed in have parameters of their own. For example, the function pipeline passes a value to one function, then takes that function's result and passes it to a second, and returns the final result:

```
const pipeline = (initial, first, second) => {
  return second(first(initial))
}
```

Let's use this to combine a function that trims blanks off the starts and ends of strings and another function that uses a **regular expression** (Appendix H) to replace spaces with dots:

```
const trim = (text) => { return text.trim() }
const dot = (text) => { return text.replace(/ /g, '.') }

const original = '  this example uses text  '

const trimThenDot = pipeline(original, trim, dot)
console.log(`trim then dot: |${trimThenDot}|`)
```

```
trim then dot: |this.example.uses.text|
```

During the call to `temp = first(initial)`, but before a value has been returned to be assigned to `temp`, memory looks like Figure 3.6. Reversing the order of the functions changes the result:

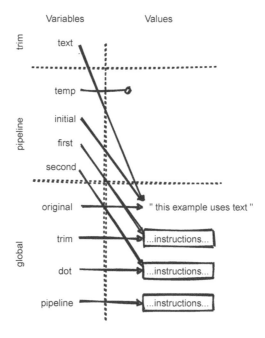

Figure 3.6: Implementing a Pipeline

```
const dotThenTrim = pipeline(original, dot, trim)
console.log(`dot then trim: |${dotThenTrim}|`)
```

```
dot then trim: |..this.example.uses.text..|
```

We can make a more general pipeline by passing an array of functions:

```
const pipeline = (initial, operations) => {
  let current = initial
  for (let op of operations) {
    current = op(current)
  }
  return current
}
```

Going through this line by line:

- The function `pipeline` takes an initial input value and array of functions. Each of those functions must take one value as an input and produce one value as output.
- We initialize a variable called `current` to hold the current value. We have to use `let` for this rather than `const` because we want to update it after each step of the pipeline runs.
- We then call each of the functions in the pipeline in turn, passing in the current value and storing the result to be passed into the next function.
- The final result is whatever came out of the last step in the pipeline.

We don't actually have to create a separate variable for the current value; since parameters are always variables rather than constants, we could just overwrite the parameter `initial` over and over again like this:

```
const pipeline = (current, operations) => {
  for (let op of operations) {
    current = op(current)
  }
  return current
}
```

Let's add a function `double` to our suite of text manglers:

```
const double = (text) => { return text + text }
```

and then try it out:

```
const original = ' some text '
const final = pipeline(original, [double, trim, dot])
console.log(`|${original}| -> |${final}|`)
```

```
| some text | -> |some.text..some.text|
```

The order of operations is:

1. `current` is assigned ` some text ` (with spaces around each word).
2. It is then assigned `double(' some text ')`, or ` some text  some text `.
3. That value is then passed to `trim`, so `'some text  some text'` (without leading or trailing spaces) is assigned to `current`.
4. Finally, the current value is passed to `dot` and the result `some.text..some.text.` is returned.

3.3 ANONYMOUS FUNCTIONS

Remember the function `oneMore`? We can pass it a value that we have calculated on the fly:

```
oneMore = (x) => {
  return x + 1
}

console.log(oneMore(3 * 2))
```

```
7
```

Behind the scenes, JavaScript allocates a nameless temporary variable to hold the value of 3 * 2, then passes a reference to that temporary variable into `oneMore`. We can do the same thing with functions, i.e., create one on the fly without giving it a name as we're passing it into some other function. For example, suppose that instead of pushing one value through a pipeline of functions, we want to call a function once for each value in an array:

```
const transform = (values, operation) => {
  let result = []
  for (let v of values) {
    result.push(operation(v))
  }
  return result
}

const data = ['one', 'two', 'three']
const upper = transform(data, (x) => { return x.toUpperCase() })
console.log(`upper: ${upper}`)
```

```
upper: ONE,TWO,THREE
```

Taking the first letter of a word is so simple that it's hardly worth giving the function a name, so let's move the definition into the call to `transform`:

```
const first = transform(data, (x) => { return x[0] })
console.log(`first: ${first}`)
```

```
first: o,t,t
```

A function that is defined where it is used and isn't assigned a name is called an **anonymous function**. Most callback functions in JavaScript are written this way: the function with the given parameters and body (in this case, x and `return x[0]`) is passed directly to something else (in this case, `transform`) to be called.

3.4 FUNCTIONAL PROGRAMMING

Functional programming is a style of programming that relies heavily on **higher-order functions** like `pipeline` that take other functions as parameters. In addition, functional programming expects that functions won't modify data in place, but will instead create new data from old. For example, a true believer in functional programming would be saddened by this:

```
// Create test array
const test = [1,2,3]

const impure = (values) => {
  for (let i in values) {
    values[i] += 1
  }
}

// Run function
impure(test)

// Original array has been modified
console.log(`test: ${test}`)

test: 2,3,4
```

and would politely but firmly suggest that it be rewritten like this:

```
const test = [1,2,3]

const pure = (values) -> {
  result = []
  for (let v of values) {
    result.push(v + 1)
  }
  return result
}

// Rather than modify test, we create a new array for the results
const newArray = pure(test)
console.log(`newArray: ${newArray}$`)
console.log(`test: ${test}`)

newArray: 2,3,4
test: 1,2,3
```

JavaScript arrays provide several methods to support functional programming. For example, `Array.some` returns `true` if *any* element in an array passes a test, while `Array.every` returns `true` if *all* elements in an array pass a test. Here's how they work:

```
const data = ['this', 'is', 'a', 'test']
console.log('some longer than 3:',
         data.some((x) => { return x.length > 3 }))
console.log('all longer than 3:',
         data.every((x) => { return x.length > 3 }))
```

```
some longer than 3: true
all longer than 3: false
```

Array.filter creates a new array containing only values that pass a test:

```
const data = ['this', 'is', 'a', 'test']
console.log('those longer than 3:',
            data.filter((x) => { return x.length > 3 }))
```

```
those longer than 3: [ 'this', 'test' ]
```

So do all of the elements with more than 3 characters start with a 't'?

```
const data = ['this', 'is', 'a', 'test']
const result = data
               .filter((x) => { return x.length > 3 })
               .every((x) => { return x[0] === 't' })
console.log(`all longer than 3 start with t: ${result}`)
```

```
all longer than 3 start with t: true
```

Array.map creates a new array by calling a function for each element of an existing array:

```
const data = ['this', 'is', 'a', 'test']
console.log('shortened', data.map((x) => { return x.slice(0, 2) }))
```

```
shortened [ 'th', 'is', 'a', 'te' ]
```

Finally, Array.reduce reduces an array to a single value using a combining function and a starting value. The combining function must take two values, which are the current running total and the next value from the array; if the array is empty, Array.reduce returns the starting value.

An example will make this clearer. To start, let's create an acronym using a loop:

```
const data = ['this', 'is', 'a', 'test']

let acronym = ''
for (let value of data) {
  acronym = acronym + value[0]
}

console.log(`acronym of ${data} is ${acronym}`)
```

```
acronym of this,is,a,test is tiat
```

The three key elements in the short program above are the input data, the initial value of the variable acronym, and the way that variable is updated. When Array.reduce is used, the array is the data and the initial value and update function are passed as parameters:

```
const data = ['this', 'is', 'a', 'test']

const concatFirst = (accumulator, nextValue) => {
  return accumulator + nextValue[0]
}
let acronym = data.reduce(concatFirst, '')
console.log(`acronym of ${data} is ${acronym}`)
```

```
acronym of this,is,a,test is tiat
```

As elsewhere, we can define the function where we use it:

```
const data = ['this', 'is', 'a', 'test']

acronym = data.reduce((accum, next) => {
  return accum + next[0]
}, '')
console.log('all in one step:', acronym)
```

```
all in one step: tiat
```

The indentation of the anonymous function defined inside reduce may look a little odd, but this is the style the JavaScript community has settled on.

3.5 CLOSURES

The last tool we need to introduce is an extremely useful side effect of the way memory is handled. The easiest way to explain it is by example. We have already defined a function called pipeline that chains any number of other functions together:

```
const pipeline = (initial, operations) => {
  let current = initial
  for (let op of operations) {
    current = op(current)
  }
  return current
}
```

However, pipeline only works if each function in the array operations has a single parameter. If we want to be able to add 1, add 2, and so on, we have to write separate functions, which is annoying.

A better option is to write a function that creates the function we want:

```
const adder = (increment) => {
  const f = (value) => {
    return value + increment
  }
  return f
}

const add_1 = adder(1)
const add_2 = adder(2)
console.log(`add_1(100) is ${add_1(100)}, add_2(100) is ${add_2(100)}`)
```

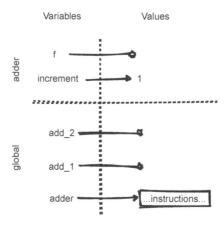

Figure 3.7: Creating an Adder (Step 1)

```
add_1(100) is 101, add_2(100) is 102
```

The best way to understand what's going on is to draw a step-by-step memory diagram. In step 1, we call adder(1) (Figure 3.7). adder creates a new function that includes a reference to that 1 we just passed in (Figure 3.8). In step 3, adder returns that function, which is assigned to add_1 (Figure 3.9). Crucially, the function that add_1 refers to still has a reference to the value 1, even though that value isn't referred to any longer by anyone else.

In steps 4–6, we repeat these three steps to create another function that has a reference to the value 2, and assign that function to add_2 (Figure 3.10).
When we now call add_1 or add_2, they add the value passed in and the value they've kept a reference to.

This trick of capturing a reference to a value inside something else is called a **closure**. It works because JavaScript holds on to values as long as anything, anywhere, still refers to them. Closures solve our pipeline problem by letting us define little functions on the fly and give them extra data to work with:

```
const result = pipeline(100, [adder(1), adder(2)])
console.log(`adding 1 and 2 to 100 -> ${result}`)
```

```
adding 1 and 2 to 100 -> 103
```

Again, adder(1) and adder(2) do not add anything to anything: they define new (unnamed) functions that add 1 and 2 respectively when called.

Programmers often go one step further and define little functions like this inline:

```
const result = pipeline(100, [(x) => x + 1, (x) => x + 2])
console.log(`adding 1 and 2 to 100 -> ${result}`)
```

```
adding 1 and 2 to 100 -> 103
```

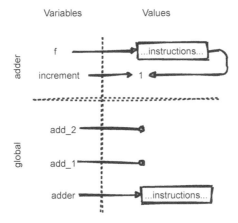

Figure 3.8: Creating an Adder (Step 2)

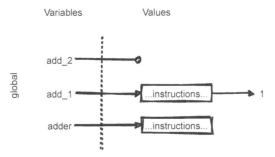

Figure 3.9: Creating an Adder (Step 3)

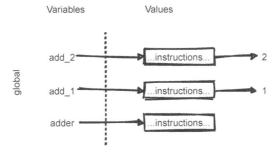

Figure 3.10: Creating an Adder (Steps 4-6)

As this example shows, if the body of a function is a single expression, it doesn't have to be enclosed in {...} and `return` doesn't need to be used.

3.6 EXERCISES

SIDE EFFECTS WITH FOREACH

JavaScript arrays have a method called `forEach`, which calls a callback function once for each element of the array. Unlike `map`, `forEach` does *not* save the values returned by these calls or return an array of results. The full syntax is:

```
someArray.forEach((value, location, container) => {
  // 'value' is the value in 'someArray'
  // 'location' is the index of that value
  // 'container' is the containing array (in this case, 'someArray')
})
```

If you only need the value, you can provide a callback that only takes one parameter; if you only need the value and its location, you can provide a callback that takes two. Use this to write a function `doubleInPlace` that doubles all the values in an array in place:

```
const vals = [1, 2, 3]
doubleInPlace(vals)
console.log(`vals after change: ${vals}`)

vals after change: 2,4,6
```

ANNOTATING DATA

Given an array of objects representing observations of wild animals:

```
data = [
  {'date': '1977-7-16', 'sex': 'M', 'species': 'NL'},
  {'date': '1977-7-16', 'sex': 'M', 'species': 'NL'},
  {'date': '1977-7-16', 'sex': 'F', 'species': 'DM'},
  {'date': '1977-7-16', 'sex': 'M', 'species': 'DM'},
  {'date': '1977-7-16', 'sex': 'M', 'species': 'DM'},
  {'date': '1977-7-16', 'sex': 'M', 'species': 'PF'},
  {'date': '1977-7-16', 'sex': 'F', 'species': 'PE'},
  {'date': '1977-7-16', 'sex': 'M', 'species': 'DM'}
]
```

write a function that returns a new array of objects like this:

```
newData = [
  {'seq': 3, 'year': '1977', 'sex': 'F', 'species': 'DM'},
  {'seq': 7, 'year': '1977', 'sex': 'F', 'species': 'PE'}
]
```

without using any loops. The changes are:

- The `date` field is replaced with just the year.
- Only observations of female animals are retained.
- The retained records are given sequence numbers to relate them back to the original data. (These sequence numbers are 1-based rather than 0-based.)

You will probably want to use `Array.reduce` to generate the sequence numbers.

KEY POINTS

- JavaScript stores the instructions making up a function in memory like any other object.
- Function objects can be assigned to variables, put in lists, passed as arguments to other functions, etc.
- Functions can be defined in place without ever being given a name.
- A callback function is one that is passed in to another function for it to execute at a particular moment.
- Functional programming uses higher-order functions on immutable data.
- `Array.some` is true if any element in an array passes a test, while `Array.every` is true if they all do.
- `Array.filter` selects elements of an array that pass a test.
- `Array.map` creates a new array by transforming values in an existing one.
- `Array.reduce` reduces an array to a single value.
- A closure is a set of variables captured during the definition of a function.

4 Objects and Classes

Making new code use old code is easy: just load the libraries you want and write calls to the functions you need. Making *old* code use *new* code without rewriting it is trickier, but **object-oriented programming** (OOP) can help.

4.1 DOING IT BY HAND

As we saw in Chapter 2, an object in JavaScript is a set of key-value pairs. Since functions are just another kind of data, an object's values can be functions, so data can carry around functions that work on it. For example, we can create an object to represent a square:

```
const square = {
  name: 'square',
  size: 5,
  area: (it) => { return it.size * it.size },
  perimeter: (it) => { return 4 * it.size }
}
```

and then pass the object itself into each of its own functions:

```
const a = square.area(square)
console.log(`area of square is ${a}`)
```

```
area of square is 25
```

This is clumsy—we'll often forget to pass the object into its functions—but it allows us to handle many different kinds of things in the same way. For example, we can create another object to represent a circle:

```
const circle = {
  name: 'circle',
  radius: 3,
  area: (it) => { return Math.PI * it.radius * it.radius },
  perimeter: (it) => { return 2 * Math.PI * it.radius }
}
```

and then put all of these different objects in an array and operate on them in the same way without knowing precisely what kind of object we're dealing with:

```
const show_all = (shapes) => {
  for (let s of shapes) {
    const a = s.area(s)
    const p = s.perimeter(s)
    console.log(`${s.name}: area ${a} perimeter ${p}`)
  }
}

show_all([square, circle])
```

```
square: area 25 perimeter 20
circle: area 28.274333882308138 perimeter 18.84955592153876
```

As long as we only use the value `name` and the functions `area` and `perimeter` we don't need to know what kind of shape we have. This is called **polymorphism**, and it allows us to add new shapes without changing the code in our loop. In other words, it allows old code (in this case, the function `show_all`) to use new code (the new object `rectangle`):

```
const rectangle = {
  name: 'rectangle',
  width: 2,
  height: 3,
  area: (it) => { return it.width * it.height },
  perimeter: (it) => { return 2 * (it.width + it.height) }
}

show_all([square, circle, rectangle])
```

```
square: area 25 perimeter 20
circle: area 28.274333882308138 perimeter 18.84955592153876
rectangle: area 6 perimeter 10
```

4.2 CLASSES

Building every object by hand and calling `thing.function(thing)` is clumsy. JavaScript solved these problems using **prototypes**, which turned out to be almost as clumsy as our hand-rolled solution (Section G.3). Most object-oriented languages use **classes** instead (Figure 4.1); these were added to JavaScript in ES6, and we will use them instead of prototypes throughout. Here's how we create a class that defines the properties of a square, without actually creating any specific squares:

```
class Square {
  constructor (size) {
    this.name = 'square'
    this.size = size
  }
  area () { return this.size * this.size }
  perimeter () { return 4 * this.size }
}
```

(Class names are written in CamelCase by convention.) We can then create a specific square by using the class's name as if it were a function:

```
const sq = new Square(3)
console.log(`sq name ${sq.name} and area ${sq.area()}`)
```

```
sq name square and area 9
```

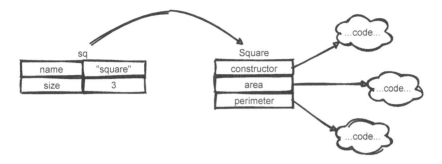

Figure 4.1: Objects and Classes in Memory

new ClassName(...) creates a new blank object and marks it to show that it is an **instance** of ClassName. Objects need to know what class they belong to so that they can find their **methods**, which are the functions defined within the class that operate on instances of it. (We'll explain how JavaScript marks objects in Section G.3; it's more complicated than it needs to be in order to be compatible with older versions of the language.)

Before new hands the newly-created object back to the program, it calls the specially-named **constructor** to initialize the object's state. Inside the constructor and other methods, the object being operated on is referred to by the pronoun this. For example, if the constructor assigns an array to this.values, then every instance of that class gets its own array.

Everything Old is New Again

Methods are defined within a class using classic function syntax rather than the fat arrows we have been using. The inconsistency is unfortunate but this way of defining methods is what the current version of Node prefers; we will explore this topic further in Chapter 8.

There are a lot of new terms packed into the preceding three paragraphs, so let's retrace the execution of:

```
const sq = new Square(3)
console.log(`sq name ${sq.name} and area ${sq.area()}`)
```

1. new creates a blank object, then looks up the definition of the class Square and calls the constructor defined inside it with the value 3.
2. Inside that call, this refers to the newly-created blank object. The constructor adds two keys to the object: name, which has the value 'square', and size, which has the value 3.
3. Once the constructor finishes, the newly-created object is assigned to the variable sq.
4. In order to create a string to pass to console.log, the program has to look up the value of sq.name, which works like looking up any other key in an object.

5. The program also has to call `sq.area`. During that call, JavaScript temporarily assigns `sq` to the variable `this` so that the `area` method can look up the value of `size` in the object it's being called for.
6. Finally, the program fills in the template string and calls `console.log`.

JavaScript classes support polymorphism: if two or more classes have some methods with the same names that take the same parameters and return the same kinds of values, other code can use objects of those classes interchangeably. For example, here's a class-based rewrite of our shapes code:

```javascript
class Circle {
  constructor (radius) {
    this.name = 'circle'
    this.radius = radius
  }
  area () { return Math.PI * this.radius * this.radius }
  perimeter () { return 2 * Math.PI * this.radius }
}

class Rectangle {
  constructor (width, height) {
    this.name = 'rectangle'
    this.width = width
    this.height = height
  }
  area () { return this.width * this.height }
  perimeter () { return 2 * (this.width + this.height) }
}

const everything = [
  new Square(3.5),
  new Circle(2.5),
  new Rectangle(1.5, 0.5)
]
for (let thing of everything) {
  const a = thing.area(thing)
  const p = thing.perimeter(thing)
  console.log(`${thing.name}: area ${a} perimeter ${p}`)
}
```

```
square: area 12.25 perimeter 14
circle: area 19.634954084936208 perimeter 15.707963267948966
rectangle: area 0.75 perimeter 4
```

4.3 INHERITANCE

We can build new classes from old ones by adding or **overriding** methods. To show this, we'll start by defining a person:

```javascript
class Person {
  constructor (name) {
    this.name = name
  }
```

```
  greeting (formal) {
    if (formal) {
      return `Hello, my name is ${this.name}`
    } else {
      return `Hi, I'm ${this.name}`
    }
  }

  farewell () {
    return `Goodbye`
  }
}
```

This class allows us to create an instance with a formal greeting:

```
const parent = new Person('Hakim')
console.log(`parent: ${parent.greeting(true)} - ${parent.farewell()}`)


parent: Hello, my name is Hakim - Goodbye
```

We can now **extend** Person to create a new class Scientist, in which case we say that Scientist **inherits** from Person, or that Person is a **parent class** of Scientist and Scientist is a **child class** of Person.

```
class Scientist extends Person {
  constructor (name, area) {
    super(name)
    this.area = area
  }

  greeting (formal) {
    return `${super.greeting(formal)}. Let's talk about ${this.area}...`
  }
}
```

This tells us that a Scientist is a Person who:

- Has an area of specialization as well as a name.
- Says hello in a slightly longer way
- Says goodbye in the same way as a Person (since Scientist *doesn't* define its own farewell method)

The word super is used in two ways here:

- In the constructor for Scientist, super(...) calls up to the constructor of the parent class Person so that it can do whatever initialization it does before Scientist does its own initialization. This saves us from duplicating steps.

- Inside `greeting`, the expression `super.greeting(formal)` means "call the parent class's `greeting` method for this object". This allows methods defined in child classes to add to or modify the behavior of methods defined in parent classes, again without duplicating code.

Let's try it out:

```
const child = new Scientist('Bhadra', 'microbiology')
console.log(`child: ${child.greeting(false)} - ${child.farewell()}`)
```

```
child: Hi, I'm Bhadra. Let's talk about microbiology... - Goodbye
```

Figure 4.2 shows what memory looks like after these classes have been defined and the objects `parent` and `child` have been created. It looks complex at first, but allows us to see how JavaScript finds the right method when `child.farewell()` is called:

- It looks in the object `child` to see if there's a function there with the right name.
- There isn't, so it follows `child`'s link to its class `Scientist` to see if a function is there.
- There isn't, so it follows the link from `Scientist` to the parent class `Person` and finds the function it's looking for.

4.4 EXERCISES

DELAYS

Define a class called `Delay` whose `call` method always returns the value given in the *previous* call:

```
const example = new Delay('a')
for (let value of ['b', 'c', 'd']) {
  console.log(value, '->', example.call(value))
}
```

```
b -> a
c -> b
d -> c
```

A class like `Delay` is sometimes called **stateful**, since it remembers its state from call to call.

FILTERING

Define a class called `Filter` whose `call` method returns `null` if its input matches one of the values given to its constructor, or the input as output otherwise:

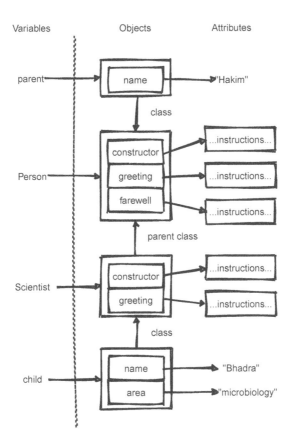

Figure 4.2: Object-Oriented Inheritance

```
const example = new Filter('a', 'e', 'i', 'o', 'u')
for (let value of ['a', 'b', 'c', 'd', 'e']) {
  console.log(value, '->', example.call(value))
}

a -> null
b -> b
c -> c
d -> d
e -> null
```

A class like Filter is sometimes called **stateless**, since it does not remember its state from call to call.

PIPELINES

Define a class called Pipeline whose constructor takes one or more objects with a single-parameter call method, and whose own call method passes a value through each of them in turn. If any of the components' `call` methods returns `null`, `Pipeline` stops immediately and returns `null`.

```javascript
const example = new Pipeline(new Filter('a', 'e', 'i', 'o', 'u'),
                            new Delay('a'))
for (let value of ['a' ,'b', 'c', 'd', 'e']) {
  console.log(value, '->', example.call(value))
}
```

```
a -> null
b -> a
c -> b
d -> c
e -> null
```

ACTIVE EXPRESSIONS

Consider this class:

```javascript
class Active {
  constructor (name, transform) {
    this.name = name
    this.transform = transform
    this.subscribers = []
  }

  subscribe (someone) {
    this.subscribers.push(someone)
  }

  update (input) {
    console.log(this.name, 'got', input)
    const output = this.transform(input)
    for (let s of this.subscribers) {
      s.update(output)
    }
  }
}
```

and this program that uses it:

```javascript
const start = new Active('start', (x) => Math.min(x, 10))
const left = new Active('left', (x) => 2 * x)
const right = new Active('right', (x) => x + 1)
const final = new Active('final', (x) => x)
start.subscribe(left)
start.subscribe(right)
left.subscribe(final)
right.subscribe(final)

start.update(123)
```

1. Trace what happens when the last line of the program is called.

2. Modify `Active` so that it calls `transform` *if* that function was provided, or a method `Active.transform` if a transformation function wasn't provided.
3. Create a new class `Delay` whose `transform` method always returns the previous value. (Its constructor will need to take an initial value as a parameter.)

This pattern is called **observer/observable**.

KEY POINTS

- Create classes to define combinations of data and behavior.
- Use the class's constructor to initialize objects.
- `this` refers to the current object.
- Use polymorphism to express common behavior patterns.
- Extend existing classes to create new ones-sometimes.
- Override methods to change or extend their behavior.

5 HTML and CSS

HTML is the standard way to represent documents for presentation in web browsers, and CSS is the standard way to describe how it should look. Both are more complicated than they should have been, but in order to create web applications, we need to understand a little of both.

5.1 FORMATTING

An HTML **document** contains **elements** and text (and possibly other things that we will ignore for now). Elements are shown using **tags**: an opening tag <tagname> shows where the element begins, and a corresponding closing tag </tagname> (with a leading slash) shows where it ends. If there's nothing between the two, we can write <tagname/> (with a trailing slash).

A document's elements must form a **tree** (Figure 5.1), i.e., they must be strictly nested. This means that if Y starts inside X, Y must end before X ends, so <X>...<Y>...</Y></X> is legal, but <X>...<Y>...</X></Y> is not. Finally, every document should have a single **root element** that encloses everything else, although browsers aren't strict about enforcing this. In fact, most browsers are pretty relaxed about enforcing any kind of rules at all, since most people don't obey them anyway.

5.2 TEXT

The text in an HTML page is normal printable text. However, since < and > are used to show where tags start and end, we must use **escape sequences** to represent them, just as we use \" to represented a literal double-quote character inside a double-quoted string in JavaScript. In HTML, escape sequences are written &name;, i.e., an ampersand, the name of the character, and a semi-colon. A few common escape sequences are shown in Table 5.1.

Name	Escape Sequence	Character
Less than	&lt;	<
Greater than	&gt;	>
Ampersand	&amp;	&
Copyright	&copy;	©
Plus/minus	&plusmn;	±
Micro	&micro;	µ

Table 5.1: HTML Escapes

The first two are self-explanatory, and & is needed so that we can write a literal ampersand (just as \\ is needed in JavaScript strings so that we can write a literal backslash). ©, ±, and µ are usually not needed any longer, since most editors will allow us to put non-ASCII characters directly into documents these days, but occasionally we will run into older or stricter systems.

5.3 PAGES

An HTML page should have:

- a single html element that encloses everything else
- a single head element that contains information about the page
- a single body element that contains the content to be displayed.

It doesn't matter whether or how we indent the tags showing these elements and the content they contain, but laying them out on separate lines and indenting to show nesting helps human readers. Well-written pages also use comments, just like code: these start with `<!--` and end with `-->`. Unfortunately, comments cannot be nested, i.e., if you comment out a section of a page that already contains a comment, the results are unpredictable.

Here's an empty HTML page with the structure described above:

```html
<html>
  <head>
    <!-- description of page goes here -->
  </head>
  <body>
    <!-- content of page goes here -->
  </body>
</html>
```

Nothing shows up if we open this in a browser, so let's add a little content:

```html
<html>
  <head>
    <title>This text is displayed in the browser bar</title>
  </head>
  <body>
    <h1>Displayed Content Starts Here</h1>
    <p>
      This course introduces core features of <em>JavaScript</em>
      and shows where and how to use them.
    </p>
    <!-- The word "JavaScript" is in italics (emphasis) in the preceding -->
      <!-- paragraph. -->
  </body>
</html>
```

- The title element inside head gives the page a title. This is displayed in the browser bar when the page is open, but is *not* displayed as part of the page itself.

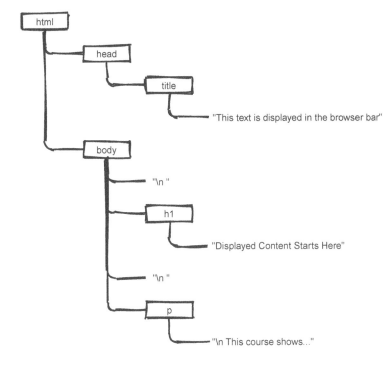

Figure 5.1: HTML as a Tree

- The h1 element is a level-1 heading; we can use h2, h3, and so on to create sub-headings.
- The p element is a paragraph.
- Inside a heading or a paragraph, we can use em to *emphasize* text. We can also use strong to make text **stronger**. Tags like these are better than tags like i (for italics) or b (for bold) because they signal intention rather than forcing a particular layout. Someone who is visually impaired, or someone using a small-screen device, may want emphasis of various kinds displayed in different ways.

5.4 ATTRIBUTES

Elements can be customized by giving them **attributes**, which are written as name="value" pairs inside the element's opening tag. For example:

```
<h1 align="center">A Centered Heading</h1>
```

centers the h1 heading on the page, while:

```
<p class="disclaimer">This planet provided as-is.</p>
```

marks this paragraph as a disclaimer. That doesn't mean anything special to HTML, but as we'll see later, we can define styles based on the `class` attributes of elements.

An attribute's name may appear at most once in any element, just like a key can only appear once in any JavaScript object, so `<p align="left" align="right">...</p>` is illegal. If we want to give an attribute multiple values—for example, if we want an element to have several classes—we put all the values in one string. Unfortunately, as the example below shows, HTML is inconsistent about whether values should be separated by spaces or semi-colons:

```
<p class="disclaimer optional" style="color: blue; font-size: 200%;">
```

However they are separated, values are supposed to be quoted, but in practice we can often get away with `name=value`. And for Boolean attributes whose values are just true or false, we can even sometimes just get away with `name` on its own.

5.5 LISTS

Headings and paragraphs are all very well, but data scientists need more. To create an unordered (bulleted) list, we use a `ul` element, and wrap each item inside the list in `li`. To create an ordered (numbered) list, we use `ol` instead of `ul`, but still use `li` for the list items.

```
<ul>
  <li>first</li>
  <li>second</li>
  <li>third</li>
</ul>
```

- first
- second
- third

```
<ol>
  <li>first</li>
  <li>second</li>
  <li>third</li>
</ol>
```

1. first
2. second
3. third

Lists can be nested by putting the inner list's `ul` or `ol` inside one of the outer list's `li` elements:

```
<ol>
  <li>Major A
    <ol>
```

```
          <li>minor p</li>
          <li>minor q</li>
        </ol>
    </li>
    <li>Major B
      <ol>
          <li>minor r</li>
          <li>minor s</li>
      </ol>
    </li>
</ol>
```

1. Major A
   1. minor p
   2. minor q
2. Major B
   1. minor r
   2. minor s

5.6 TABLES

Lists are a great way to get started, but if we *really* want to impress people with our data science skills, we need tables. Unsurprisingly, we use the `table` element to create these. Each row is a `tr` (for "table row"), and within rows, column items are shown with `td` (for "table data") or `th` (for "table heading").

```
<table>
  <tr> <th>Alkali</th>    <th>Noble Gas</th> </tr>
  <tr> <td>Hydrogen</td> <td>Helium</td>     </tr>
  <tr> <td>Lithium</td>  <td>Neon</td>        </tr>
  <tr> <td>Sodium</td>   <td>Argon</td>       </tr>
</table>
```

Alkali	Noble Gas
Hydrogen	Helium
Lithium	Neon
Sodium	Argon

Do *not* use tables to create multi-column layouts: there's a better way.

5.7 LINKS

Links to other pages are what make HTML hypertext (Figure 5.2). Confusingly, the element used to show a link is called `a`. The text inside the element is displayed and (usually) highlighted for clicking. Its `href` attribute specifies what the link is pointing at; both local filenames and URLs are supported. Oh, and we can use `<br/>`

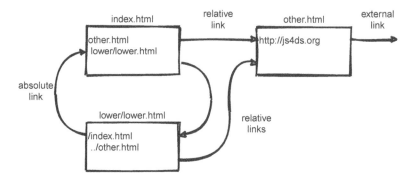

Figure 5.2: Pages and Links

to force a line break in text (with a trailing slash inside the tag, since the br element doesn't contain any content):

```
<a href="https://nodejs.org/">Node.js</a>
<br/>
<a href="https://facebook.github.io/react/">React</a>
<br/>
<a href="../index.html">home page (relative path)</a>
```

This appears as:

```
Node.js
React
home page (relative path)
```

with the usual clickability.

5.8 IMAGES

Images can be stored inside HTML pages in two ways: by using SVG (which we will discuss in Chapter 8) or by encoding the image as text and including that text in the body of the page, which is clever, but makes the source of the pages very hard to read.

It is far more common to store each image in a separate file and refer to that file using an img element (which also allows us to use the image in many places without copying it). The src attribute of the img tag specifies where to find the file; as with the href attribute of an a element, this can be either a URL or a local path. Every img should also include a title attribute (whose purpose is self-explanatory) and an alt attribute with some descriptive text to aid accessibility and search engines. (Again, we have wrapped and broken lines so that they will display nicely in the printed version.)

```
<img src="./assets/logo.png" title="Book Logo"
    alt="Displays the book logo using a local path" />
<img src="https://js4ds.org/assets/logo.png"
    title="Book Logo"
    alt="Display the book logo using a URL" />
```

Two things to note here are:

1. Since img elements don't contain any text, they are often written with the trailing-slash notation. However, they are also often written improperly as <img src="..."> without any slashes at all. Browsers will understand this, but some software packages will complain.
2. If an image file is referred to using a path rather than a URL, that path can be either **relative** or **absolute**. If it's a relative path, it's interpreted starting from where the web page is located; if it's an absolute path, it's interpreted relative to wherever the web browser thinks the **root directory** of the filesystem is. As we will see in Chapter 12, this can change from one installation to the next, so you should always try to use relative paths, except where you can't. It's all very confusing...

5.9 CASCADING STYLE SHEETS

When HTML first appeared, people styled elements by setting their attributes:

```
<html>
  <body>
    <h1 align="center">Heading is Centered</h1>
    <p>
      <b>Text</b> can be highlighted
      or <font color="coral">colorized</font>.
    </p>
  </body>
</html>
```

Many still do, but a better way is to use **Cascading Style Sheets** (CSS). These allow us to define a style once and use it many times, which makes it much easier to maintain consistency. (We were going to say "...and keep pages readable", but given how complex CSS can be, that's not a claim we feel we can make.) Here's a page that uses CSS instead of direct styling:

```
<html>
  <head>
    <link rel="stylesheet" href="simple-style.css" />
  </head>
  <body>
    <h1 class="title">Heading is Centered</h1>
    <p>
      <span class="keyword">Text</span> can be highlighted
      or <span class="highlight">colorized</span>.
    </p>
  </body>
</html>
```

The `head` contains a link to an **external style sheet** stored in the same directory as the page itself; we could use a URL here instead of a relative path, but the `link` element *must* have the `rel="stylesheet"` attribute. Inside the page, we then set the `class` attribute of each element we want to style.

The file `simple-style.css` looks like this:

```
h1.title {
  text-align: center;
}
span.keyword {
  font-weight: bold;
}
.highlight {
  color: coral;
}
```

Each entry has the form `tag.class` followed by a group of properties inside curly braces, and each property is a key-value pair. We can omit the class and just write (for example):

```
p {
  font-style: italic;
}
```

in which case the style applies to everything with that tag. If we do this, we can override general rules with specific ones: the style for a disclaimer paragraph is defined by p with overrides defined by `p.disclaimer`. We can also omit the tag and simply use `.class`, in which case every element with that class has that style.

As suggested by the earlier discussion of separators, elements may have multiple values for class, as in `<span class="keyword highlight">...</span>`. (The `span` element simply marks a region of text, but has no effect unless it's styled.)

These features are one (but unfortunately not the only) common source of confusion with CSS: if one may override general rules with specific ones but also provide multiple values for class, how do we keep track of which rules will apply to an element with multiple classes? A detailed discussion of the order of precedence for CSS rules is outside the scope of this tutorial. We recommend that those likely to work often with stylesheets read (and consider bookmarking) this W3Schools page[1].

One other thing CSS can do is match specific elements. We can label particular elements uniquely within a page using the `id` attribute, then refer to those elements using `#name` as a **selector**. For example, if we create a page that gives two spans unique IDs:

```
<html>
  <head>
    <link rel="stylesheet" href="selector-style.css" />
  </head>
```

---

[1]https://www.w3schools.com/css/css_specificity.asp

```
  <body>
    <p>
      First <span id="major">keyword</span>.
    </p>
    <p>
      Full <span id="minor">explanation</span>.
    </p>
  </body>
</html>
```

then we can style those spans like this:

```
#major {
  text-decoration: underline red;
}
#minor {
  text-decoration: overline blue;
}
```

Internal Links

We can link to an element in a page using #name inside the link's href: for example, <a href="page.html#place">text</a> refers to the #place element in page.html. This is particularly useful within pages: <a href="#place">jump</a> takes us straight to the #place element within this page. Internal links like this are often used for cross-referencing and to create a table of contents.

5.10 BOOTSTRAP

CSS can become very complicated very quickly, so most people use a framework to take care of the details. One of the most popular is Bootstrap[2] (which is what we use to style our website). Here's the entire source of a page that uses Bootstrap to create a two-column layout with a banner at the top (Figure 5.3):

```
<html>
  <head>
    <link rel="stylesheet"
        href="https://stackpath.bootstrapcdn.com/bootstrap/\
            4.1.3/css/bootstrap.min.css">
    <style>
      div {
        border: solid 1px;
      }
    </style>
  </head>
  <body>

    <div class="jumbotron text-center">
```

---

[2]https://getbootstrap.com/

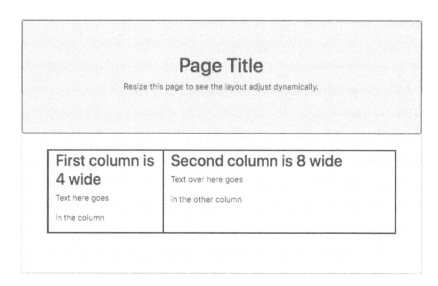

Figure 5.3: Bootstrap Layout

```
   <h1>Page Title</h1>
   <p>Resize this page to see the layout adjust dynamically.</p>
 </div>

 <div class="container">
   <div class="row">
     <div class="col-sm-4">
       <h2>First column is 4 wide</h2>
       <p>Text here goes</p>
       <p>in the column</p>
     </div>
     <div class="col-sm-8">
       <h2>Second column is 8 wide</h2>
       <p>Text over here goes</p>
       <p>in the other column</p>
     </div>
   </div>
 </div>

 </body>
</html>
```

The page opens by loading Bootstrap from the web; we can also download `bootstrap.min.css` and refer to it with a local path. (The `.min` in the file's name signals that the file has been **minimized** so that it will load more quickly.)

The page then uses a `style` element to create an **internal style sheet** to put a solid one-pixel border around every `div` so that we can see the regions of the page more clearly. Defining styles in the page header is generally a bad idea, but it's a good way to test things quickly. Oh, and a `div` just marks a region of a page without doing anything to it, just as a `span` marks a region of text without changing its appearance unless we apply a style.

The first div creates a header box (called a "jumbotron") and centers its text. The second div is a container, which creates a bit of margin on the left and right sides of our content. Inside that container is a row with two columns, one 4/12 as wide as the row and the other 8/12 as wide. (Bootstrap uses a 12-column system because 12 has lots of divisors.)

Bootstrap is **responsive**: elements change size as the page grows narrower, and are then stacked when the screen becomes too small to display them side by side.

We've left out many other aspects of HTML and CSS as well, such as figure captions, multi-column table cells, and why it's so hard to center text vertically within a div. One thing we will return to in Chapter 10 is how to include interactive elements like buttons and forms in a page. Handling those is part of why JavaScript was invented in the first place, but we need more experience before tackling them.

5.11 EXERCISES

CUTTING CORNERS

What does your browser display if you forget to close a paragraph or list item tag like this:

```
<p>This paragraph starts but doesn't officially end.

<p>Another paragraph starts here but also doesn't end.

<ul>
  <li>First item in the list isn't closed.
  <li>Neither is the second.
</ul>
```

1. What happens if you don't close a ul or ol list?
2. Is that behavior consistent with what happens when you omit </p> or </li>?

MIX AND MATCH

1. Create a page that contains a 2x2 table, each cell of which has a three-item bullet-point list. How can you reduce the indentation of the list items within their cells using CSS?
2. Open your page in a different browser (e.g., Firefox or Edge). Do they display your indented lists consistently?
3. Why do programs behave inconsistently? Why do programmers do this to us? Why? Why why why why why?

NAMING

What does the sm in Bootstrap's col-sm-4 and col-sm-8 stand for? What other options could you use instead? Why do web developers still use FORTRAN-style names in the 21st Century?

COLOR

HTML and CSS define names for a small number of colors. All other colors must be specified using **RGB** values. Write a small JavaScript program that creates an HTML page that displays the word `color` in 100 different randomly-generated colors. Compare this to the color scheme used in your departmental website. Which one hurts your eyes less?

UNITS

What different units can you use to specify text size in CSS? What do they mean? What does *anything* mean, when you get right down to it?

KEY POINTS

- HTML is the latest in a long line of markup languages.
- HTML documents contain elements (represented by tags in angle brackets) and text.
- Elements must be strictly nested.
- Elements can contain attributes.
- Use escape sequences beginning with ampersand to represent special characters.
- Every page should have one `html` element containing a `head` and a `body`.
- Use `<!--...-->` to include comments in HTML.
- Use `ul` and `ol` for unordered and ordered lists, and `li` for list elements.
- Use `table` for tables, `tr` for rows, `th` for headings, and `td` for regular data.
- Use `<a href="...">...</a>` to create links.
- Use `<img src="..." title="..." alt="..." />` to include images.
- Use CSS to define appearance of elements.
- Use `class` and `id` to identify elements.
- Use selectors to specify the elements that CSS applies to.

6 Manipulating Pages

We have presented a lot of tools, but as yet no applications. As a reward for your patience, we will therefore work through several examples that show how to do useful things to web pages. These examples introduce some new concepts, the most important of which is the way in which HTML pages are represented in, and manipulated by, JavaScript.

One thing these examples *don't* show is how to build interactive web pages. JavaScript was invented primarily to support buttons, forms, and the like, but we will need a bit more background before exploring them. Still, we can do a surprising number of useful things simply by playing with the content of pages.

6.1 COUNTING PARAGRAPHS

Let's begin by counting the number of paragraphs in a page:

```
<html>
  <head>
    <meta charset="utf-8"/>
  </head>
  <body>
    <h1>Title</h1>
    <div id="fill"></div>
    <h2 id="one">First <em>emphasized</em></h2>
    <p>stuff</p>
    <h2 id="two">Second <code>with code</code></h2>
    <h3>stuff</h3>
    <h2 id="three">Third</h2>
    <p>stuff</p>

    <script>
      const counter = () => {
        const paragraphs = document.querySelectorAll('p')
        return paragraphs.length
      }
      console.log(`number of paragraphs: ${counter()}`)
    </script>
  </body>
</html>
```

This page has three main parts:

1. The head contains a meta tag that specifies the page's **character encoding**, i.e., the scheme used to represent characters not found on a standard American keyboard in the 1970s. Character sets and character encodings are out of scope for

this lesson; see this essay[1] for an unfortunately timeless discussion.
2. The top half of the body has some headings and paragraphs for the JavaScript to play with. It also contains a div marked with class="fill" that our script will eventually fill in with a count.
3. The script itself is contained in a script tag at the bottom of the page; we will explore it in depth below.

When Scripts Run

We have put the script at the bottom of the page because we want to be sure that the page's contents actually exist in memory before trying to process them. If we put the script *tag and its contents at the top of the page, the browser might run our JavaScript* after *the page has been read but* before *its elements and text have been parsed and stored in memory.* **Race conditions** *like this bedevil web programming; we will see more robust ways to deal with them later.*

Inside the script tag, we define a function called counter that takes no arguments, then use console.log to display the result of calling it. The only thing inside the function that we haven't encountered before is the call document.querySelectorAll('p'). As you might guess from its name, document is an object that gives us a handle on the page the script is in; it is created and provided automatically by the browser. Its querySelectorAll method finds all elements in the page that match the selector we provide. In this case, we're looking for all paragraphs, so we simply search for 'p'.

To see the JavaScript in action, run a browser, open its developer tools so that you can see the JavaScript console, and then load the page. The page's elements will be displayed as usual, and the console will show:

```
number of paragraphs: 2
```

Developer Tools

To open developer tools in Firefox, go to the main menu and select Tools > Web Developer > Toggle Tools. *A tabbed display will open in the bottom of your page; choose* Console *to view the output of your JavaScript, or to write a little bit to run immediately. You can open a similar set of tools from* View > Developer > JavaScript Console *in Chrome, or by using* Ctrl+Shift+I *on Windows for Firefox, Chrome, or Microsoft Edge.*

Showing results in the console is good enough for development work, but we would like to see the result in the page itself. To do this, we can replace the call to console.log with the two lines shown below:

---

[1]https://www.joelonsoftware.com/2003/10/08/the-absolute-minimum-every-software-developer-
absolutely-positively-must-know-about-unicode-and-character-sets-no-excuses/

```
const counter = () => {
  const paragraphs = document.querySelectorAll('p')
  return paragraphs.length
}
const fill = document.getElementById('fill')
fill.innerHTML = `number of paragraphs: ${counter()}`
```

Where document.querySelectorAll returns all nodes that match a selector, document.getElementById returns a single element that has the specified ID (which is set inside the element's opening tag with id="some_name"). The variable fill is therefore assigned a reference to our div. We can then change the text inside that element by assigning to its innerHTML property. When we do this, JavaScript parses the string we provided as if it were HTML and creates whatever nodes it needs to represent the result. In this case, the content is just text, so JavaScript will create a single text node, store "number of paragraphs: 2" as its content, and add it to the in-memory structure that represents the page.

...at which point some magic happens behind the scenes. The browser stores the elements and text of the current page in a data structure called the Document Object Model, or more commonly the **DOM**. As shown in Figure 5.1, the DOM is organized as a tree: each element or piece of text is a **node** in the tree, and a node's children are the elements contained within it. Any time the browser detects a change to the DOM, it automatically refreshes just as much of its display as it needs to. We can insert or remove text, change elements' styles, or copy in entire sub-pages: each time, the browser will do only the work required to reflect that change as quickly as possible.

6.2 CREATING A TABLE OF CONTENTS

Reporting the number of paragraphs is a good way to see how JavaScript works in the browser, but isn't particularly useful (although counting the number of words is—we will tackle that in the exercises). Something we're more likely to put in a real page is a table of contents, which takes only a little more code than what we've already seen:

```
(() => {
  const container = document.getElementById('fill')
  const headings = Array.from(document.querySelectorAll('h2'))
  const items = headings
        .map((h) => `<li><a href="#${h.id}">${h.innerHTML}</a></li>`)
        .join('')
  container.innerHTML = '<ul>' + items + '</ul>'
})()
```

Let's start with the first and last lines, since they demonstrate a commonly-used idiom. We've seen how to define a function and then call it:

```
const f = (param) => {
  // body
}
f()
```

If we're only going to call the function once, we might as well define it and call it immediately without giving it a name:

```
(param) => {
  // body
}(actual_value)
```

However, this doesn't reliably work as written; in order to make JavaScript happy, we have to put parentheses around the function definition so that it's clear exactly what's being called:

```
((param) => {
  // body
})(actual_value)
```

() before the fat arrow means "this function doesn't take any parameters". The second () after the closing curly brace means "call the function". If the function doesn't take any arguments, this becomes:

```
(() => {
  // body
})()
```

which is a lot of parentheses in a row, but that's what people write.

Let's come back to the body of the function:

```
const container = document.getElementById('fill')
const headings = Array.from(document.querySelectorAll('h2'))
const items = headings
      .map((h) => `<li><a href="#${h.id}">${h.innerHTML}</a></li>`)
      .join('')
container.innerHTML = '<ul>' + items + '</ul>'
```

As before, the first line gets the `div` we're going to fill in. The second line grabs all the h2 headings, which we have arbitrarily decided are the only things worthy of inclusion in the table of contents. We run the result of `document.querySelectorAll` through the function `Array.from` because the former's result isn't a JavaScript array: for reasons that probably made sense to someone, somewhere, it's a thing called a `NodeList` that lacks most of `Array`'s useful methods.

Static Methods

*`Array.from` is a **static method**: it belongs to the class as a whole, not to objects of that class. Static methods are primarily used to associate utility functions with classes, like `dist` in the example below. Unlike calls to **instance methods** like `magnitude`, static methods are called using `class.method()` rather than `some_object.method()`.*

We then have three lines that do most of the function's work. The first tells us that `items` is going to be assigned something derived from `headings`; the second transforms the array of headings into an array of strings, and the third joins those strings to create a single string. Looking at the map call, each heading becomes a list item (li) containing a link (a) whose href attribute is the ID of the heading and whose displayed content (the text between <a...> and </a>) is the text of the heading. The href attribute's value starts with #, which makes this a local link (i.e., it links to something inside the same page). If one of our h2 headings doesn't have an id set, this map will fail; we'll explore ways to handle this in the exercises.

Finally, the last line of the code shown above fills in the content of the container (i.e., the div) with an unordered list (ul) that contains all of the items we just constructed. Again, when we assign to an element's innerHTML property, JavaScript parses the string we give it and constructs the HTML nodes we need. It would be marginally faster to build these nodes ourselves (which we will do in the exercises), but building and parsing strings is usually easier to read, and the performance differences are small enough in modern browsers that we should only worry about them if they actually prove themselves a problem.

6.3   SORTABLE LISTS

Creating nodes allows us to add content to a page, but we can also rearrange the nodes that are there (Figure 6.1). Our next exercise is to sort the elements of a list, so that if the author writes:

```
<ul>
  <li>pee (P)</li>
  <li>cue (Q)</li>
  <li>are (R)</li>
</ul>
```

we will automatically rearrange the items to be:

```
<ul>
  <li>are (R)</li>
  <li>cue (Q)</li>
  <li>pee (P)</li>
</ul>
```

Our first attempt uses this as the HTML page:

```
<html>
  <head>
    <meta charset="utf-8">
    <script src="sort-lists.js"></script>
  </head>

  <body onload="sortLists()">

    <ul class="sorted">
      <li>first</li>
      <li>second</li>
```

```
  <li>third</li>
  <li>fourth</li>
  <li>fifth</li>
</ul>

<ol class="sorted">
  <li>one</li>
  <li>two</li>
  <li>three</li>
  <li>four</li>
  <li>five</li>
</ol>

</body>
</html>
```

and this as our initial script:

```
const sortLists = () => {
  const allLists = Array.from(document.querySelectorAll('#sorted'))
  lists.forEach((list) => {
    const children = Array.from(list.childNodes)
          .filter(c => c.nodeName !== '#text')
    children.sort((left, right) =>
                left.textContent.localeCompare(right.textContent))
    while (list.firstChild) {
      list.removeChild(list.firstChild)
    }
    children.forEach(c => list.appendChild(c))
  })
}
```

When we load the page, though, the items aren't sorted. A bit of trial and error
reveals that we have tripped over the race condition alluded to earlier: if we call our
function in the onload attribute of the body tag, it is run when the page is loaded
into memory but *before* the page's content has been parsed and turned into a DOM
tree. After searching online for "run JavaScript when page loaded", we go back to
this:

```
<html>
  <head>
    <meta charset="utf-8">
    <script src="sort-lists-event.js"></script>
  </head>

  <body>
    ...lists as before...
  </body>
</html>
```

and write our JavaScript like this:

```
const sortLists = () => {
  // ...function to sort lists...
```

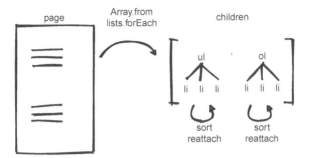

Figure 6.1: Sorting and Replacing

```
}

document.addEventListener("DOMContentLoaded", (event) => {
  sortLists()
})
```

An **event listener** is a function that the browser calls when some kind of event occurs. In our example, the event we care about is "DOM content has been loaded". When that occurs, the browser will call sortLists(). (The event parameter to our function will be given an object that stores details about what precisely happened. We don't need that information now, but will use it later when we start handling button clicks and the like.)

Let's return to the function:

```
const sortLists = () => {
  const lists = Array.from(document.querySelectorAll('.sorted'))
  lists.forEach((list) => {
    const children = Array.from(list.childNodes)
          .filter(c => c.nodeName !== '#text')
    children.sort((left, right) =>
                left.textContent.localeCompare(right.textContent))
    while (list.firstChild) {
      list.removeChild(list.firstChild)
    }
    children.forEach(c => list.appendChild(c))
  })
}
```

As before, it starts by creating an array containing the nodes we want to operate on. (We use the selector .sorted (with a leading dot) to select everything with the class sorted, rather than #sorted, which would find nodes with the ID sorted.) This array will then have all the ul or ol lists that the function is to sort.

We process each list separately with lists.forEach. The callback function inside forEach uses Array.from to create an array containing the child nodes of the main list element, then filters that list to remove any that are text nodes. We need the `Array.from` call because (once again) the DOM doesn't use a JavaScript array to store children, but a structure of its own devising that lacks the methods we want to call. We remove the text nodes because they represent the **whitespace** between list elements, such as newline characters after a closing `</li>` and before the next opening `<li>`.

Identifying Text Nodes

We could check `c.nodeType` *instead of* `c.nodeName` *to spot text nodes, but we felt that* `nodeName` *made the code easier to understand. As always, we use* `!==` *for the comparison in order to prevent unpleasant surprises (Section G.1).*

Now that we have an array of the `li` elements to be sorted, we can use `Array.sort` to order them. Since we want to sort them by the text they contain, we have to provide our own sorting function that returns a negative number, 0, or a positive number to show whether its `left` argument is less than, equal to, or greater than its `right` argument. We use the `textContent` member of the node to get the text it contains, and the string object's `localeCompare` to get a -1/0/1 result. All of this was discovered by searching online, primarily on the W3Schools[2] site.

Unfortunately, searching for "remove all children from node" tells us that we have to do it ourselves, so we use a `while` loop to remove all the children (including the unwanted top-level text elements) from the `ul` or `ol` list, then add all of the children back in sorted order. Sure enough, the page now displays the nodes in the right order.

6.4 BIBLIOGRAPHIC CITATIONS

And so we come to the largest example in this lesson. HTML has a `cite` tag for formatting citations, but it doesn't allow us to link directly to a bibliography entry. In order to minimize typing in scholarly papers, we'd like to find links like this:

```
<a href="#b">key1, key2</a>
```

and turn them into this:

```
[<a href="../bib/#key1">key1</a>, <a href="../bib/#key2">key2</a>]
```

The typed-in form is about as little typing as we can get away with; the displayed form then wraps the citations in `[...]` and turns each individual citation into a link to our bibliography. For now, we'll assume that the bibliography can be found at `../bib/`, i.e., in a file called `index.html` that's in a directory called `bib` that's a sibling of the directory containing whatever page the citation is in. This is very fragile, and we should be ashamed of ourselves, but we can tell ourselves that we're going to fix it later and get on with learning JavaScript for now.

Our test page contains two bibliographic links and one non-bibliographic link:

---

[2]https://www.w3schools.com/

```
<html>
  <head>
    <meta charset="utf-8">
    <script src="citations.js"></script>
  </head>
  <body>

    <p>As <a href="#b">Moreau1896</a> shows...</p>
    <p>
      We can look to <a href="#b">Brundle1982, Brundle1984</a>
      for answers.
    </p>
    <hr/>
    <p><em>Visit <a href="http://somewhere.org">the author's site</a>.</em></p>

  </body>
</html>
```

Here's our function (Figure 6.2), which we'll call from an event listener as before:

```
const citations = () => {
  Array.from(document.querySelectorAll('a'))
    .filter(link => link.getAttribute('href') === '#b')
    .map(link => (
      {node: link,
       text: link.textContent.split(',').map(s => s.trim())}
    ))
    .map(({node, text}) => (
      {node,
       text: text.map(cite => `<a href="../bib/#${cite}">${cite}</a>`)}
    ))
    .map(({node, text}) => (
      {node,
       text: `[${text.join(', ')}]`}
    ))
    .forEach(({node, text}) => {
      const span = document.createElement('span')
      span.innerHTML = text
      node.parentNode.replaceChild(span, node)
    })
}
```

There is a lot going on here, but it all uses patterns we have seen before. It starts by building an array of all the links in the document i.e., every a element:

```
Array.from(document.querySelectorAll('a'))
// output:
// - <a href="#b">Moreau1896</a>
// - <a href="#b">Brundle1982, Brundle1984</a>
// - <a href="http://somewhere.org">the author's site</a>
```

(We show the nodes in comments to visualize what each step of the pipeline does.) We then filter this array to find the links pointing at #b, which is what we're using to signal citations:

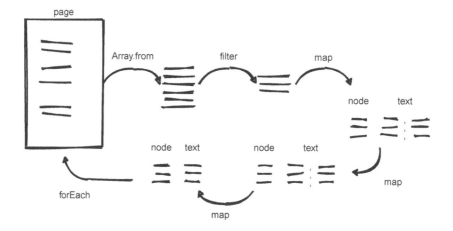

Figure 6.2: A Processing Pipeline

```
.filter(link => link.getAttribute('href') === '#b')
// output:
// - <a href="#b">Moreau1896</a>
// - <a href="#b">Brundle1982, Brundle1984</a>
```

We now have a problem. We could use a map call to get the text out of each link
and process it, but then all we'd have is an array of strings. We're going to want the
nodes those strings came out of later on as well so that we can modify their href
attributes, so somehow we have to pass the nodes and strings together through our
pipeline. One option would be to create a two-element array for each:

```
.map(link => [link, link.textContent.whatever])
```

but it's more readable to create an object so that each component has a name:

```
.map(link => (
  {node: link,
   text: link.textContent.split(',').map(s => s.trim())}
))
// output:
// - {node: <a href="#b">Moreau1896</a>,
//    text: ['Moreau1896']}
// - {node: <a href="#b">Brundle1982, Brundle1984</a>,
//    text: ['Brundle1982', 'Brundle1984']}
```

Here, we are turning each link into an object whose "node" key has the link's
DOM node as its value, and whose "text" key has the node's text, which we split
on commas and trim to remove leading and trailing whitespace.

But we're not done looking at this stage of our pipeline:

1. We don't need to quote the names "node" and "text", though we could.

2. JavaScript's `String.split` returns an array, so the value associated with `"text"` is an array. We then `map` over its elements to trim leading and trailing space from each.

3. If we wrote `link => {node: link, text: whatever}`, JavaScript would interpret the curly braces `{...}` as meaning, "Here is the body of a function," and then complain because what's in those curly braces clearly *isn't* a function body. Putting parentheses around the curly braces, i.e., writing `({...})`, tells JavaScript that the function is returning an object.

After all of this, the next stage of the pipeline is almost a relief:

```
.map(({node, text}) => (
  {node,
   text: text.map(cite => `<a href="../bib/#${cite}">${cite}</a>`)}
))
// output:
// - {node: <a href="#b">Moreau1896</a>,
//    text: [<a href="../bib/#Moreau1896">Moreau1896</a>]}
// - {node: <a href="#b">Brundle1982, Brundle1984</a>,
//    text: [<a href="../bib/#Brundle1982">Brundle1982</a>,
//           <a href="../bib/#Brundle1984">Brundle1984</a>]}
```

All right, that's not actually much of a relief, but it does make a strange kind of sense. First, if we have an object whose keys are called a and b, then the call f({a, b}) means, "Match the value of key a to a parameter called a and the value of key b to a parameter called b." This is called **destructuring**, and can save a lot of wear and tear on our keyboard and eyes.

Second, if we have a variable called name, then define an object with {name}, JavaScript helpfully assumes that what we mean is {"name": name}, i.e., that we want a key called "name" with whatever value name currently has. This allows us to pass the value of node from call to call in our pipeline without typing anything more than its name.

And after all of *this*, the `text.map` call actually *is* a relief. The value associated with the key text is an array of strings, each of which is a bibliography key. All the map does is convert each to the text we want: a link that refers to `../bib/#citation_key` and whose displayed text is also the citation key.

On to the next stage, which joins the string in text together to create a single string with commas between the entries and square brackets around the whole thing:

```
.map(({node, text}) => (
  {node,
   text: `[${text.join(', ')}]`}
))
```

(We haven't shown the output in commas because typesetting it would overflow the page and because our pseudo-HTML notation gets really confusing once we're showing strings containing HTML that contain strings.)

The last stage in our pipeline uses `forEach` instead of `map` because we want to do something for each element of the array, but don't need a value returned (because what we're doing has the side effect of modifying the document):

```
.forEach(({node, text}) => {
  const span = document.createElement('span')
  span.innerHTML = text
  node.parentNode.replaceChild(span, node)
})
```

This is the point at which carrying the node itself forward through the pipeline pays off. We create a `span` element, fill it in by assigning to its `innerHTML` property, and then replace the original link node with the node we have just created. If we now add an event listener after our function to call it when the page is loaded, we see our citations formatted as we desired.

6.5 A REAL-TIME CLOCK

We will wrap up this lesson with an example that is short, but hints at the possibilities to come:

```
<html>
  <head>
    <script>
      const startTime = () => {
        const today = new Date()
        const fields = [today.getHours(),
                        today.getMinutes(),
                        today.getSeconds()]
        const current = fields
              .map(t => `${t}`.padStart(2, '0'))
              .join(':')
        document.getElementById('current').innerHTML = current
        setTimeout(startTime, 1000)
      }

      document.addEventListener("DOMContentLoaded", (event) => {
        startTime()
      })
    </script>
  </head>

  <body>
    <p id="current"></p>
  </body>
</html>
```

Defining a function: check. Calling that function when the DOM is ready: check. What about inside the function? It's pretty easy to guess that `Date()` creates an object that holds a date, and from the fact that we're assigning that object to a variable called `today`, you might even guess that if we don't specify which date we want, we get today's values. We then pull the hours, minutes, and seconds out of the date and put them in an array so that we can turn each value into a two-character string, padded with a leading zero if necessary, and then join those strings to create a time like `17:48:02` to stuff into the element whose ID is `current`.

But what does `setTimeout` do? It tells the browser to run a function after some number of milliseconds have passed. In this case, we're running the same function `startTime` a second from now. That call will change the displayed time, then set up another callback to run a second later, and so on forever. When we load the page, we see the current time updating itself second by second to remind us just how quickly life is passing by.

6.6 EXERCISES

WHAT ENCODING IS THIS?

1. Write a function that looks up the character encoding of the page the script is in and prints it to the console.
2. Extend the function to look up all the `meta` tags in the current page and print their names and values.

WORD COUNT

1. Write a function called `countWords` that finds all the text nodes in a page, splits them on whitespace, and returns the total number of words in the page.
2. Write a second function called `showWords` that uses the first to find the number of words, then displays that number in a paragraph whose ID is `wordcount`.

A MORE ROBUST TABLE OF CONTENTS

1. What does the table of contents example generate if an `h2` *doesn't* have an `id` attribute?
2. Modify the example so that it only includes `h2` elements that have an `id` attribute in the table of contents.

EXPLICITLY CREATING NODES

Find documentation online for the two functions `document.createElement` and `document.createTextNode`, then rewrite the table of contents example to use these methods (and any others like them that you need) instead of assigning to a node's `innerHTML` property.

KEY POINTS

- Use a `meta` tag in a page's header to specify the page's character encoding.
- Pages are represented in memory using a Document Object Model (DOM).
- The `document` object represents the page a script is in.

- Use the `querySelectorAll` method to find DOM nodes that match a condition.
- Assign HTML text to a node's `innerHTML` property to change the node's content.
- Use `((params) => {...})(arguments)` to create and call a function in a single step.
- An event listener is a function run by the browser when some specific event occurs.
- Create an event listener for `'DOMContentLoaded'` to trigger execution of scripts *after* the DOM has been constructed.
- Check the `nodeType` or `nodeName` property of a DOM node to find out what kind of node it is.
- Destructuring assignment allows us to assign to multiple variables by name in a single statement.
- Use `setTimeout` to trigger execution of a function after a delay.
- To make something run forever, have the function called by `setTimeout` set another timeout of the same function.

7 Dynamic Pages

In the beginning, people created HTML pages by typing them in (just as we have been doing). They quickly realized that a lot of pages share a lot of content: navigation menus, contact info, and so on. The nearly universal response was to create a **template** and embed commands to include other snippets of HTML (like headers) and loop over data structures to create lists and tables. This is called **server-side page generation**: the HTML is generated on the **server**, and it was popular because that's where the data was, and that was the only place complex code could be run. (This tutorial uses a templating tool called Jekyll[1]. It's clumsy and limited, but it's the default on GitHub[2].)

Server-side generation can be done statically or dynamically, i.e., pages can be compiled once, stored on disk, and served thereafter, or each page can be recompiled whenever it's needed, which makes it easy to include dynamic elements like today's top news story (Figure 7.1).

As browsers and JavaScript became more powerful, the balance shifted toward **client-side page generation**. In this model, the browser fetches data from one or more servers and feeds that data to a JavaScript library that generates HTML in the browser for display. This allows the **client** to decide how best to render data, which is increasingly important as phones and tablets take over from desktop and laptop computers. It also moves the computational burden off the server and onto the client device, which lowers the cost of providing data.

Many (many) JavaScript frameworks for client-side page generation have been created, and more are probably being developed right now. We have chosen React[3] because it is freely available, widely used, well documented, simpler than many alternatives, and has a cool logo. Its central design principles are:

1. Page creators use functions to describe the HTML they want.
2. They then let React decide which functions to run when data changes.

We will show how to use it in pure JavaScript, then introduce a tool called JSX that simplifies things.

7.1   HELLO, WORLD

Let's begin by saying hello:

---

[1] https://jekyllrb.com/

[2] http://github.com/

[3] https://reactjs.org/

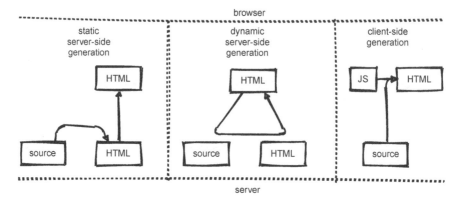

Figure 7.1: Page Generation Alternatives

```
<!DOCTYPE html>
<html>
  <head>
    <meta charset="utf-8">
    <title>Hello React</title>
    <script src="https://fb.me/react-15.0.1.js"></script>
    <script src="https://fb.me/react-dom-15.0.1.js"></script>
  </head>
  <body>
    <div id="app">
      <!-- this is filled in -->
    </div>
    <script>
      ReactDOM.render(
        React.DOM.h1(null, "Hello React"),
        document.getElementById("app")
      )
    </script>
  </body>
</html>
```

The head of the page loads two React libraries from the web; we will use locally-installed libraries later. The body contains a div with an ID to make it findable. When our script runs, React will put the HTML it generates into this div.

The script itself creates an h1 with the text "Hello, React" using React.DOM.h1, then finds the document element whose ID is "app" and uses ReactDOM.render to insert the former into the latter. This alters the representation of the page in memory, not the source of the page on disk; if we want to inspect the resulting HTML, we have to do so in the browser. Finally, we put the script at the bottom of the page so that the browser will have turned the HTML into a DOM tree in memory before the script runs. We will come back and fix this later.

Inspection Tools

If you are using the Firefox browser, you can open the developer tools pane by going to the main menu and selecting Tools... Web Developer... Toggle Tools. *A tabbed display will open in the bottom of your page; choose* Inspector *to view the content of your page and page's CSS. As you move your mouse around the page itself, corresponding structural elements will be highlighted. It's actually pretty cool. . .*

The first parameter to React.DOM.h1 is null in the example above, but it can more generally be an object that specifies the attributes we want the newly-created node to have. There are a few quirks in this—for example, we have to use fontStyle rather than font-style so that the attribute object's keys look like legal JavaScript variables—but the mechanism is seductively easy to use:

```
<body>
  <div id="app"></div>
  <script>
    const attributes = {
      'style': {
        'background': 'pink',
        'fontStyle': 'italic'
      }
    }
    ReactDOM.render(
      React.DOM.h1(attributes, "Hello Stylish"),
      document.getElementById("app")
    )
  </script>
</body>
```

7.2 JSX

Writing nested functions is a clumsy way to write HTML, so most React programmers use a tool called JSX[4] that translates HTML into JavaScript function calls. And yes, those JavaScript function calls then produce HTML—it's a funny world. Here's an example:

```
<!DOCTYPE html>
<html>
  <head>
    <meta charset="utf-8">
    <title>Hello JSX</title>
    <script src="https://fb.me/react-15.0.1.js"></script>
    <script src="https://fb.me/react-dom-15.0.1.js"></script>
    <script src="https://unpkg.com/babel-standalone@6/babel.js"></script>
  </head>
  <body>
    <div id="app"></div>
    <script type="text/babel">
```

---

[4]https://reactjs.org/docs/introducing-jsx.html

```
    ReactDOM.render(
      <h1>Hello JSX</h1>,
      document.getElementById('app')
    )
  </script>
 </body>
</html>
```

Along with the two React libraries, this page includes a tool called Babel[5] to translate a mix of HTML and JavaScript into pure JavaScript. To trigger translation, we add the attribute `type="text/babel"` to the `script` tag.

Why bother? Because as the example above shows, it allows us to write `<h1>Hello JSX</h1>` instead of calling a function. More generally, JSX lets us put JavaScript inside our HTML (inside our JavaScript (inside our HTML)), so we can (for example) use `map` to turn a list of strings into an HTML list:

```
<body>
  <h1>JSX List</h1>
  <div id="app"></div>
  <script type="text/babel">
    const allNames = ['McNulty', 'Jennings', 'Snyder',
                      'Meltzer', 'Bilas', 'Lichterman']
    ReactDOM.render(
      <ul>{allNames.map((name) => <li>{name}</li> )}</ul>,
      document.getElementById('app')
    )
  </script>
</body>
```

We have to use `map` rather than a loop because whatever code we run has to return something that can be inserted into the DOM, and `for` loops don't return anything. (We could use a loop to build up a string through repeated concatenation, but `map` is cleaner.) And note: we must return exactly one node, because this is one function call. We will look in the exercises at why the curly braces immediately inside the `<ul>` element are necessary.

Note also that when we run this, the browser console will warn us that each list element ought to have a unique `key` property, because React wants each element of the page to be selectable. We will add this later.

7.3 CREATING COMPONENTS

One of the most powerful features of React is that it lets us create new **components** that look like custom HTML tags, but are associated with functions that we write. React requires the names of these components to start with a capital letter to differentiate them from regular tags. We can, for example, define a function `ListOfNames` to generate our list of names, then put that element directly in `ReactDOM.Render` just as we would put an `h1` or `p`:

---

[5]https://babeljs.io/

```
<body>
  <h1>Create Component</h1>
  <div id="app"></div>
  <script type="text/babel">
    const allNames = ['McNulty', 'Jennings', 'Snyder',
                      'Meltzer', 'Bilas', 'Lichterman']

    const ListOfNames = () => {
      return (<ul>{allNames.map((name) => <li>{name}</li> )}</ul>)
    }

    ReactDOM.render(
      <ListOfNames />,
      document.getElementById('app')
    )
  </script>
</body>
```

What we really want to do, though, is pass parameters to these components: after all, JSX is turning them into functions, and functions are far more useful when we can give them data. In React, all the attributes we put inside the component's tag are passed to our function in a single props object:

```
<body>
  <h1>Pass Parameters</h1>
  <div id="app"></div>
  <script type="text/babel">
    const allNames = ['McNulty', 'Jennings', 'Snyder',
                      'Meltzer', 'Bilas', 'Lichterman']

    const ListElement = (props) =>
        (<li id={props.name}><em>{props.name}</em></li>)

    ReactDOM.render(
      <ul>{allNames.map((name) => <ListElement name={name} /> )}</ul>,
      document.getElementById('app')
    )
  </script>
</body>
```

If you look carefully, you'll see that the name attribute passed to the use of ListElement becomes the value of prop.names inside the function that implements ListElement.

Before we map each component of our array within ReactDOM.render as in the examples above, the ListElement function gives us exactly one logical place to set attributes. Here we've used ListElement to italicize each element in our array and give them ids, but these functions can also be used for any transformation or calculation on each element to be rendered.

7.4   DEVELOPING WITH PARCEL

Putting all of the source for an application in one HTML file is a bad practice, but we've already seen the race conditions that can arise when we load JavaScript in a page's header. And what about `require` statements? The browser will try to load the required files when those statements run, but who is going to serve them?

The solution is to use a **bundler** (Figure 7.2) to combine everything into one big file, and to run a **local server** to preview our application during development. However, this solution brings with it another problem: which bundler to choose? As with front-end frameworks, there are many to choose from, and new ones are being added almost weekly. Webpack[6] is probably the most widely used, but it is rather complex, so we will use Parcel[7], which is younger and therefore not yet bloated (but give it time).

Initiate a Project with Node Package Manager

If you've been coding along, so far we've created single HTML and JavaScript files, and we've used the Node command to run JavaScript files in the terminal, but we have not yet used the Node Package Manager npm. Before we install Parcel, we can turn the directory which we've been creating our HTML and JavaScript files into a project by typing:
`$ npm init -y`

To install Parcel, run:

```
$ npm install parcel-bundler
```

Once Parcel is installed, we can tell it to run one of our test pages like this:

```
$ node_modules/.bin/parcel serve -p 4000 src/dynamic/pass-params.html

Server running at http://localhost:4000
+ Built in 128ms.
```

Quitting Parcel
To leave Parcel use the keyboard interrupt Control-C.

This works because when NPM installs a library in a project's `node_modules` directory, that library may put a runnable script in `node_modules/.bin` (note that it's `.bin` with a leading `.`, not `bin`). When we ask Parcel to serve an application, it:

 • looks in the named file to find JavaScript,
 • looks recursively at what that file loads,
 • copies some files into a directory called `./dist` (which stands for "distribution"), and
 • serves the application out of there.

Parcel also caches things in `./.cache` so that it doesn't need to do redundant work; both directories are normally added to `.gitignore`. To learn more about Parcel, see this short tutorial[8].

---

[6]https://webpack.js.org/

[7]https://parceljs.org/

[8]https://medium.com/codingthesmartway-com-blog/getting-started-with-parcel-197eb85a2c8c

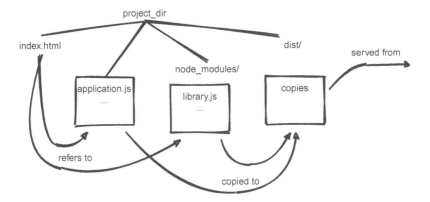

Figure 7.2: What Goes Where with Parcel

It's very common to put tasks like "run my application" into NPM's package.json file, just as older programmers would put frequently-used commands into a project's Makefile. Look for the section in package.json whose key is "scripts" and add this:

```
"scripts": {
  "dev": "parcel serve -p 4000",
  ...
},
```

We can now use npm run dev -- src/dynamic/pass-params.html, since everything after -- is passed to the script being run. This doesn't just save us typing; it also gives other developers a record of how to use the project. Unfortunately, there is no standard way to add comments to a JSON file...

Whoops

Note: if we accidentally specify the name of a directory like src/dynamic *instead of the name of an HTML file, Parcel prints an error on the console saying "no entries found". This happens because it is trying to read the directory itself as a file.*

7.5   MULTIPLE FILES

Now that we can bundle things up, let's move our JSX into app.js and load that in the head of the page:

```
<!DOCTYPE html>
<html>
  <head>
    <meta charset="utf-8">
    <title>Hello Separate</title>
    <script src="https://fb.me/react-15.0.1.js"></script>
```

```
    <script src="https://fb.me/react-dom-15.0.1.js"></script>
    <script src="https://unpkg.com/babel-standalone@6/babel.js"></script>
    <script src="app.js" type="text/babel"></script>
  </head>
  <body>
    <h1>Hello Separate</h1>
    <div id="app"></div>
  </body>
</html>
```

For now, the JavaScript in `app.js` is:

```
ReactDOM.render(
  <p>Rendered by React</p>,
  document.getElementById("app")
)
```

When we load this page we get the h1 title but *not* the paragraph. The browser console displays the message:

```
Error: _registerComponent(...): Target container is not a DOM element.
```

This is the same race condition that has bitten us before. After sighing in frustration and making another cup of tea, we decide that to keep things simple we will load the script in the body of the page:

```
<!DOCTYPE html>
<html>
  <head>
    <meta charset="utf-8">
    <title>Hello Bottom</title>
  </head>
  <body>
    <h1>Hello Bottom</h1>
    <div id="app"></div>
    <script src="./app.js" type="text/babel"></script>
  </body>
</html>
```

Installing React and ReactDOM

Now that we have made a project folder using `npm init` *and have created a* `project.json` *file, we can install our first modules:*

```
$ npm install react
$ npm install reactDOM
```

In general, uses of the function `require` *indicate that we need to install that library to access the module's functions.*

More importantly, we will rewrite `app.js` so that it loads the libraries it needs, because there's no guarantee that libraries loaded in `head` will be available when `app.js` runs:

```
const React = require('react')
const ReactDOM = require('react-dom')

ReactDOM.render(
  <p>Rendered by React</p>,
  document.getElementById('app')
)
```

We don't have to shut down the server and restart it every time we make changes like this, because Parcel watches for changes in files and relaunches itself as needed. Each time it does so, it looks at the libraries `app.js` loads and rebundles what it needs: right now, for example, `dist/app.ef6b320b.js` is 19930 lines long.

A more modern option than loading in the bottom is to add the `async` attribute to the script in the head of the page, which tells the browser not to do anything with the JavaScript until the page has finished building:

```
<!DOCTYPE html>
<html>
  <head>
    <meta charset="utf-8">
    <title>Hello Parcel</title>
    <script src="./app.js" type="text/babel" async></script>
  </head>
  <body>
    <div id="app"></div>
  </body>
</html>
```

7.6 EXERCISES

THOSE DAMN CURLY BRACES

Our list-building example includes this line of code:

```
<ul>{allNames.map((name) => <li>{name}</li> )}</ul>,
```

Why are the curly braces immediately inside the <ul> element necessary? What happens if you take them out?

REAL DATA

1. Create a file called `programmers.js` that defines a list of JSON objects called `programmers` with `firstName` and `lastName` fields for our programmers. (You can search the Internet to find their names.)
2. Load that file in your page like any other JavaScript file.
3. Delete the list `allNames` from the application and modify it to use data from the list `programmers` instead.

Loading constant data like this is a common practice during testing.

ORDERING

What happens if you change the order in which the JavaScript files are loaded in your web page? For example, what happens if you load `app.js` *before* you load `ListElement.js`?

MULTIPLE TARGETS

What happens if your HTML page contains two `div` elements with `id="app"`?

CREATING A COMPONENT FOR NAMES

Create a new React component that renders a name, and modify the example to use it instead of always displaying names in `<li>` elements.

STRIPING

Suppose we want to render every second list element in italics. (This would be a horrible design, but once we start creating tables, we might want to highlight alternate rows in different background colors to make it easier to read.) Modify the application so that even-numbered list elements are `<li>{name}</li>` and odd-numbered list elements are `<li><em>{name}</em></li>`. (Hint: use the fact that a `map` callback can have two parameters instead of one.)

KEY POINTS

- Older dynamic web sites generated pages on the server.
- Newer dynamic web sites generate pages in the client.
- React is a JavaScript library for client-side page generation that represents HTML elements as function calls.
- React replaces page elements with dynamically-generated content in memory (not on disk).
- React functions can be customized with elements.
- JSX translates HTML into React function calls so that HTML and JavaScript can be mixed freely.
- Use Babel to translate JSX into JavaScript in the browser.
- Define new React components with a pseudo-HTML element and a corresponding function.
- Attributes to pseudo-HTML are passed to the JavaScript function as a `props` object.

8 Visualizing Data

Tables and lists are great, but visualizations are often more effective—if they're well designed and your audience is sighted, that is. There are even more ways to visualize data in the browser than there are front-end toolkits for JavaScript. We have chosen to use Vega-Lite[1], which is a **declarative** framework: as a user, you specify the data and settings, and let the library take care of everything else. It doesn't do everything, but it does common things well and easily, and it interacts nicely with React.

8.1 VEGA-LITE

Let's start by creating a skeleton web page to hold our visualization. For now, we will load Vega, Vega-Lite, and Vega-Embed from the web; we'll worry about local installation later. We will create a div to be filled in by the visualization—we don't have to give it the ID vis, but it's common to do so—and we will leave space for the script. Our skeleton looks like this (with lines broken for the benefit of the printed version):

```
<!DOCTYPE html>
<html>
<head>
  <title>Embedding Vega-Lite</title>
  <script src="https://cdn.jsdelivr.net/npm/vega@5"></script>
  <script src="https://cdn.jsdelivr.net/npm/vega-lite@3"></script>
  <script src="https://cdn.jsdelivr.net/npm/vega-embed@4"></script>
</head>
<body>

  <div id="vis"></div>

  <script type="text/javascript">
  </script>
</body>
</html>
```

We can now start filling in the script with the beginning of a visualization specification. This is a blob of **JSON** with certain required fields:

- $schema identifies the version of the spec being used (as a URL).
- description is a comment to remind us what we thought we were doing when we created this.
- data is the actual data.

---

[1] http://vega.github.io/

```
...rest of page as before...
  <script type="text/javascript">
    let spec = {
      "$schema": "https://vega.github.io/schema/vega-lite/v2.0.json",
      "description": "Create data array but do not display anything.",
      "data": {
        "values": [
          {"a": "A", "b": 28},
          {"a": "B", "b": 55},
          {"a": "C", "b": 43},
          {"a": "D", "b": 91},
          {"a": "E", "b": 81},
          {"a": "F", "b": 53},
          {"a": "G", "b": 19},
          {"a": "H", "b": 87},
          {"a": "I", "b": 52}
        ]
      }
    }
  </script>
...rest of page as before...
```

In this case, we represent a two-dimensional data table as objects with explicit indices "a" and "b". We have to do this because JSON (like JavaScript) doesn't have a native representation of two-dimensional arrays with row and column headers.

Once we have created our spec, we can call `vegaEmbed` with the ID of the element that will hold the visualization, the spec, and some options (which for now we will leave empty):

```
let spec = {
  "$schema": "https://vega.github.io/schema/vega-lite/v2.0.json",
  "description": "Create data array but do not display anything.",
  "data": {
    "values": [
      // ...as above...
    ]
  }
}
vegaEmbed("#vis", spec, {})
```

When we open the page, though, nothing appears, because we haven't told Vega-Lite *how* to display the data. To do that, we need to add two more fields to the spec:

• `mark` specifies the visual element used to show the data
• `encoding` tells Vega how to map values to marks

Here's our updated spec:

```
let spec = {
  "$schema": "https://vega.github.io/schema/vega-lite/v2.0.json",
  "description": "Add mark and encoding for data.",
  "data": {
```

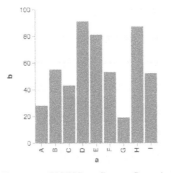

Figure 8.1: Mark and Encoding

```
    "values": [
      // ...as above...
    ]
  },
  "mark": "bar",
  "encoding": {
    "x": {"field": "a", "type": "ordinal"},
    "y": {"field": "b", "type": "quantitative"}
  }
}
vegaEmbed("#vis", spec, {})
```

When we open the page now, we see a bar chart, and feel very proud of ourselves (Figure 8.1).

There are also some poorly-styled links for various controls that we're not going to use. We can fill in the options argument to vegaEmbed to turn those off:

```
let spec = {
  "$schema": "https://vega.github.io/schema/vega-lite/v2.0.json",
  "description": "Disable control links.",
  "data": {
    // ...as before...
  }
}
let options = {
  "actions": {
    "export": false,
    "source": false,
    "editor": false
  }
}
vegaEmbed("#vis", spec, options)
```

We now have the visualization we wanted (Figure 8.2).

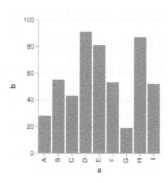

Figure 8.2: Without Controls

Vega-Lite has a *lot* of options: for example, we can use points and average the Y values. (We will change the X data so that values aren't distinct in order to show this off, because otherwise averaging doesn't do much.) In our revised spec, x is now "nominal" instead of "ordinal" and y has an extra property "aggregate", which is set to "average" (but can be used to specify other **aggregation functions**):

```
let spec = {
  "$schema": "https://vega.github.io/schema/vega-lite/v2.0.json",
  "description": "Disable control links.",
  "data": {
    "values": [
      {"a": "P", "b": 19},
      {"a": "P", "b": 28},
      {"a": "P", "b": 91},
      {"a": "Q", "b": 55},
      {"a": "Q", "b": 81},
      {"a": "Q", "b": 87},
      {"a": "R", "b": 43},
      {"a": "R", "b": 52},
      {"a": "R", "b": 53}
    ]
  },
  "mark": "point",
  "encoding": {
    "x": {"field": "a", "type": "nominal"},
    "y": {"field": "b", "type": "quantitative", "aggregate": "average"}
  }
}
let options = {
  ...disable controls as before...
}
vegaEmbed("#vis", spec, options)
```

Figure 8.3 shows the result.

Figure 8.3: Aggregating and Using Points

8.2 LOCAL INSTALLATION

Loading Vega from a **Content Delivery Network** (CDN) reduces the load on our server, but prevents offline development. Since we want to be able to work when we're disconnected, let's load from local files.

Step 1 is to slim down our HTML file so that it only loads our application:

```
<!DOCTYPE html>
<html>
  <head>
    <title>Load Vega from a File</title>
    <meta charset="utf-8">
    <script src="app.js" async></script>
  </head>
  <body>
    <div id="vis"></div>
  </body>
</html>
```

In step 2, we npm install vega vega-lite vega-embed and require('vega-embed') in app.js:

```
const vegaEmbed = require('vega-embed')

const spec = {
  // ...as before...
}

const options = {
  // ...as before...
}

vegaEmbed("#vis", spec, options)
```

We launch this with Parcel via our saved npm run command:

```
$ npm run dev -- src/vis/react-01/index.html
```

Our hearts break when we open `http://localhost:4000` in our browser and nothing appears. Looking in the browser console, we see a message telling us that `vegaEmbed` is not a function.

What we have tripped over is a leftover from JavaScript's evolution. The old method of getting libraries is `require`, and that's still what Node supports as of Version 10.9.0. The new standard is `import`, which allows a module to define a default value so that `import 'something'` gets a function, a class, or whatever. This is really handy, but `require` doesn't work that way.

We can either add the `--experimental-modules` flag when using Node on the command line, or rename our files with a `.mjs` extension, both of which are annoying. Alternatively, we can get the thing we want by accessing `.default` during import, or by referring to `vegaEmbed.default` when we call it. These choices are also annoying, but after a bit of fiddling and cursing, we decide to make the fix as the library is loaded:

```
const vegaEmbed = require('vega-embed').default

// ...as before...
```

The third option is to use `import` where we can and fix the `require` statements in the server-side code when Node is upgraded. We can call the thing we import anything we want, but we will stick to `vegaEmbed` for consistency with previous examples:

```
import vegaEmbed from 'vega-embed'

// ...as before...
```

If we do this, the bundled file is 74.5K lines of JavaScript, but at least it's all in one place for distribution.

8.3 EXERCISES

BINNED SCATTERPLOTS

Vega-Lite can create binned scatterplots[2] in which the sizes of markers indicate how many values were put in each bin. Modify the aggregating scatterplot shown above so that values are binned in this way.

GROUPED BAR CHARTS

Vega-Lite can display grouped bar charts[3] as well as simple ones. Find or create a simple dataset and construct a grouped bar chart. How impressed will your supervisor, your committee, or a future employee be by your chosen color scheme?

---

[2]https://vega.github.io/vega-lite/examples/circle_binned.html

[3]https://vega.github.io/vega-lite/examples/bar_grouped.html

LIMITS OF DECLARATIVE PROGRAMMING

Look at Vega-Lite's example gallery[4] and identify one kind of plot or transformation you've used or seen that *isn't* included there. Do you think this is because they just haven't gotten around to it yet, or is there something about that plot or transformation that doesn't lend itself to Vega-Lite's declarative model?

WORKING WITH ARRAYS

Vega-Lite is built on top of a visualization toolkit called D3[5], which includes a library for manipulating arrays[6]. Write a small application that generates 1000 random values using `Math.random` and reports the mean, standard deviation, and quartiles. (You may also want to create a histogram showing the distribution of values.)

KEY POINTS

- Vega-Lite is a simple way to build common visualizations.
- Vega-Lite is declarative: the user creates a data structure describing what they want, and the library creates the visualization.
- A Vega-Lite specification contains a schema identifier, a description, data, marks, and encodings.
- The overall layout of a Vega-Lite visualization can be controlled by setting options.
- Some applications will use `require` for server-side code and `import` for client-side code.

---

[4] https://vega.github.io/vega-lite/examples/

[5] https://d3js.org/

[6] https://github.com/d3/d3-array

9 Promises

By now we have got used to providing callback functions as arguments to other functions. Callbacks quickly become complicated because of:

- Nesting: a delayed calculation may need the result of a delayed calculation that needs...
- Error handling: who notices and takes care of errors? (This is often a problem in real life too.)

For example, suppose we want to turn a set of CSV files into HTML pages. The inputs to our function are the name of a directory that contains one or more CSV files and the name of an output directory; the desired results are that the output directory is created if it doesn't already exist, that one HTML file is created for each CSV file, that any HTML files in the directory that *don't* correspond to CSV files are removed, and that an index page is created with links to all the pages.

We can do this with synchronous operations, but that's not the JavaScript way (by which we mean that doing it that way won't introduce you to tools we're going to need later). We can also try doing it with callbacks, but:

- we can't create the output directory until the existing one has been emptied;
- can't generate the HTML pages until the output directory has been re-created; and
- we can't generate the index page until the CSV files have been processed.

Instead of a tangled nest of callbacks, it's better to use **promises**, and then to use `async` and `await` to make things even easier. JavaScript offers three mechanisms because its developers have invented better ways to do things as the language has evolved, but the simple high-level ideas often don't make sense unless you understand how they work. (This too is often a problem in real life.)

9.1 THE EXECUTION QUEUE

In order for any of what follows to make sense, it's vital to understand JavaScript's **event loop**, a full explanation of which can be found here[1]. Most functions execute in order:

```
[1000, 1500, 500].forEach(t => {
  console.log(t)
})
```

---

[1] https://nodejs.org/en/docs/guides/event-loop-timers-and-nexttick/

```
1000
1500
500
```

However, a handful of built-in functions delay execution: instead of running right away, they add a callback to a list that the JavaScript interpreter uses to keep track of things that want to be run. When one task finishes, the interpreter takes the next one from this queue and runs it.

setTimeout is one of the most widely used functions of this kind. Here it is in operation:

```
[1000, 1500, 500].forEach(t => {
  console.log(`about to setTimeout for ${t}`)
  setTimeout(() => {console.log(`inside handler for ${t}`)}, t)
})

about to setTimeout for 1000
about to setTimeout for 1500
about to setTimeout for 500
inside handler for 500
inside handler for 1000
inside handler for 1500
```

That's not surprising: if we ask JavaScript to delay execution, execution is delayed. What may be surprising is that setting a timeout of zero also defers execution:

```
const values = [1000, 1500, 500]
console.log('starting...')
values.forEach(t => {
  console.log(`about to setTimeout for ${t}`)
  setTimeout(() => {console.log(`inside handler for ${t}`)}, 0)
})
console.log('...finishing')

starting...
about to setTimeout for 1000
about to setTimeout for 1500
about to setTimeout for 500
...finishing
inside handler for 1000
inside handler for 1500
inside handler for 500
```

Figure 9.1 shows what the run queue looks like just before the program prints ...finishing. We can use setTimeout to build a generic non-blocking function:

```
const nonBlocking = (callback) => {
  setTimeout(callback, 0)
}

['a', 'b', 'c'].forEach(val => {
```

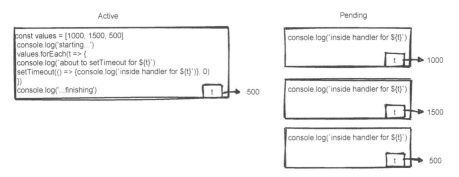

Figure 9.1: Run Queue

```
console.log(`about to do nonBlocking for ${val}`)
nonBlocking(() => console.log(`inside callback for ${val}`))
})
```

```
about to do nonBlocking for a
about to do nonBlocking for b
about to do nonBlocking for c
inside callback for a
inside callback for b
inside callback for c
```

Why bother doing this? Because we may want to give something else a chance to run. In particular, file I/O and anything involving a network request are incredibly slow from a computer's point of view. If a single CPU cycle was one second long[2], then getting data from RAM would take several minutes, getting it from a solid-state disk would take six to eight days, and getting it over the network is the equivalent of eight years. Rather than wasting that time, JavaScript is designed to let us (or our browser) switch tasks and do something else.

Using a timeout of zero is a clever trick, but Node provides another function called setImmediate to do this for us. (There is also process.nextTick, which doesn't do quite the same thing. You should probably not use it.)

```
['a', 'b', 'c'].forEach(val => {
  console.log(`about to do setImmediate for ${val}`)
  setImmediate(() => console.log(`inside immediate handler for ${val}`))
})
```

```
about to do setImmediate for a
about to do setImmediate for b
about to do setImmediate for c
inside immediate handler for a
inside immediate handler for b
inside immediate handler for c
```

---

[2]http://exple.tive.org/blarg/2018/08/15/time-dilation/

9.2 PROMISES

Recent versions of JavaScript encourage programmers to use promises to manage delayed actions. For example, if we want to find the size of a file, we can write this:

```
const fs = require('fs-extra')
fs.stat('moby-dick.txt').then((stats) => console.log(stats.size))
```

```
1276201
```

`fs-extra.stat` will eventually produce some statistics about the file, but this will take a while, so `fs-extra.stat` returns an object of the class `Promise` right away. `Promise` has a method `then` that takes a callback as an argument and stores it in the promise object. When the `stat` call completes, the remembered callback is called, and passed yet another object with statistics about the file (including its size).

To understand this a little better, let's create our own promise to fetch a file from the web. (We have broken the URL over two lines using string concatenation so that it will print nicely.)

```
const fetch = require('node-fetch')

url = 'https://api.nasa.gov/neo/rest/v1/feed' +
      '?api_key=DEMO_KEY&start_date=2018-08-20'
const prom = new Promise((resolve, reject) => {
  fetch(url)
  .then((response) => {
    if (response.status === 200) {
      resolve('fetched page successfully')
    }
  })
}).then((message) => console.log(message))
```

This code constructs a new `Promise` object. The constructor takes one argument; this must be a callback function of two arguments, which by convention are called `resolve` and `reject`. Inside the body of the callback, we call `resolve` to return a value if and when everything worked as planned. That value is then passed to the `then` method of the `Promise`.

This may seem a roundabout way of doing things, but it solves several problems at once. The first and most important is error handling: if something goes wrong inside the callback passed to `Promise`'s constructor, we can call `reject` instead of `resolve`. Just as `then` handles whatever we pass to `resolve`, `Promise` defines a method called `catch` to handle whatever is passed to `reject`. We can therefore build a slightly more robust version of our data fetcher that will report something sensible if we mis-type a month as 80:

```
const fetch = require('node-fetch')

url = 'https://api.nasa.gov/neo/rest/v1/feed' +
      '?api_key=DEMO_KEY&start_date=2018-80-20'
new Promise((resolve, reject) => {
```

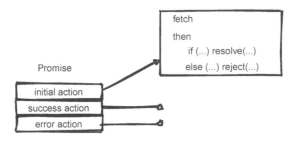

Figure 9.2: Promises as Objects (after creation)

```
fetch(url)
.then((response) => {
  if (response.status === 200) {
    resolve('fetched page successfully')
  }
  else {
    reject(Error(`got HTTP status code ${response.status}`))
  }
})
}).then((message) => console.log(message))
.catch((error) => console.log(error.message))
```

```
got HTTP status code 400
```

Note that we didn't assign our Promise object to a variable in the example above. We can create promises on the fly if we need them only to define behavior on successful completion/exception and won't need to refer to them again later.

What makes this all work is that a promise is an object. Figure 9.2 shows what's in memory just after this promise has been created. There are a lot of arrows in this diagram, but they all serve a purpose:

- The promise has three fields: the initial action (which is the callback passed to the constructor), the action to be taken if everything succeeds, and the action to be taken if there's an error.
- The success and error actions are empty, because the initial action hasn't executed yet.

Once the promise is created, the program calls its then and catch methods in that order, giving each a callback. This happens *before* the callback passed to the constructor (i.e., the initial action) is executed, and leaves the promise in the state shown in Figure 9.3:

Calling then and catch assigns callbacks to the success action and error action members of the promise object. Those methods are then passed into the initial action callback as resolve and reject, i.e., if resolve is called because the page was fetched successfully, what's actually called is the promise's success action, which is

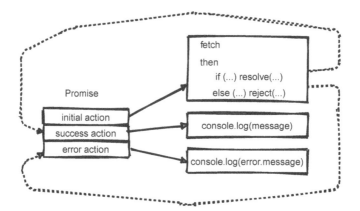

Figure 9.3: Promises as Objects (after then and catch)

the callback that was given to `then`. If `reject` is called, on the other hand, it triggers execution of the error action, which is the callback that was passed to `catch`.

Yes, this is complicated—so complicated that another layer (which we will look at in Section 9.4) has been added to JavaScript to hide these details. Without this complexity, though, it's extremely difficult to handle errors from delayed computations. If we run this using JavaScript's `try {...} catch {...}` syntax for handling exceptions:

```
const fetch = require('node-fetch')

url = 'https://api.nasa.gov/neo/rest/v1/feed' +
      '?api_key=DEMO_KEY&start_date=2018-80-20' // illegal date
try {
  fetch(url)
}
catch (err) {
  console.log(err)
}
```

then the error message won't appear because the function `fetch` is asynchronous, which means that code executes in this order:

1. inside try, ask the computer to execute `fetch(url)` at some point in the future
2. since asking this doesn't cause an exception, skip the catch
3. then run `fetch(url)`, which fails without anything in place to catch the exception because the `try...catch` has already finished so `console.log` never runs and the error message doesn't appear.

There are two passes of execution in this block: The first is the `try...catch` event loop, and the second is `fetch`. JavaScript rips the asynchronous code right out

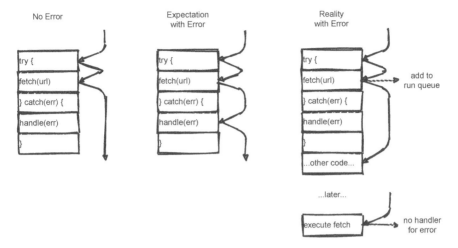

Figure 9.4: When Try...Catch Fails

of the execution context! There's no error, because `fetch` hasn't yet had the chance to run.

Going back to the `fs-extra.stat` example above, what if we want to process multiple files, for example to calculate their total size? We could write a loop:

```
const fs = require('fs-extra')

let total_size = 0
const files = ['jane-eyre.txt', 'moby-dick.txt',
               'life-of-frederick-douglass.txt']
for (let fileName of files) {
  fs.stat(fileName).then((stats) => {
    total_size += stats.size
  })
}
console.log(total_size)
```

but this doesn't work: the `stat` in each iteration is executed asynchronously, so the loop finishes and the script prints a total size of zero before any of the promised code has run.

Plan B is to chain the promises together to ensure that each executes only after the last has resolved:

```
const fs = require('fs-extra')

let total_size = 0
new Promise((resolve, reject) => {
  fs.stat('jane-eyre.txt').then((jeStats) => {
    fs.stat('moby-dick.txt').then((mdStats) => {
      fs.stat('life-of-frederick-douglass.txt').then((fdStats) => {
        resolve(jeStats.size + mdStats.size + fdStats.size)
```

```
    })
  })
 })
}).then((total) => console.log(total))
```

but this obviously doesn't handle an arbitrary number of files, since we have to write one level of nesting for each file. It's also potentially inefficient, since we could be waiting for one promise to complete while other promises further down are ready to be processed.

The answer is `Promise.all`, which returns an array of results from completed promises after all of them have resolved. The order of results corresponds to the order of the promises in the input array, which makes processing straightforward:

```
const fs = require('fs-extra')

let total_size = 0
const files = ['jane-eyre.txt', 'moby-dick.txt',
               'life-of-frederick-douglass.txt']
Promise.all(files.map(f => fs.stat(f))).
  then(stats => stats.reduce((total, s) => {return total + s.size}, 0)).
  then(console.log)
```

```
2594901
```

In future, we might also find an opportunity to use `Promise.race`, which takes an array of promises and returns the result of the first one to complete.

9.3   USING PROMISES

Promises don't really make sense until we start to use them, so let's try counting the number of lines in a set of files that are larger than a specified threshold. This is a slightly complex example but we will go through and build it up step-by-step.

Before we begin, we will want the name of the directory to search for files. We could put this in our code, but it's a lot more convenient if we allow users to provide it as a command-line argument when they run our script. To aid this, we'll use the property within Node called `process.argv` which is an array containing all the command line arguments passed to the script.

If we put this line in a file called `echo.js`:

```
console.log('arguments are:', process.argv)
```

and run it like this:

```
$ node src/promises/echo.js first second third
```

the output is:

```
arguments are: [ '/usr/local/bin/node',
  '/Users/stj/js4ds/src/promises/echo.js',
  'first',
  'second',
  'third' ]
```

The full path to Node is the first argument, the name of our script is the second, and all of the extra arguments provided by the users follow that. If we want the first of those, we therefore need process.argv[2].

The first step in counting lines is now to find the input files:

```
const fs = require('fs-extra')
const glob = require('glob-promise')

const srcDir = process.argv[2]

glob(`${srcDir}/**/*.txt`)
  .then(files => console.log('glob', files))
  .catch(error => console.error(error))
```

If we go into the directory src/promises and run:

```
$ node step-01.js .
```

to run the program with the current working directory . as its only argument, then the output is:

```
glob [ './common-sense.txt',
  './jane-eyre.txt',
  './life-of-frederick-douglass.txt',
  './moby-dick.txt',
  './sense-and-sensibility.txt',
  './time-machine.txt' ]
```

Step 2 is to get the status of each file. This approach doesn't work because fs.stat is delayed:

```
// ...imports and arguments as before...

glob(`${srcDir}/**/*.txt`)
  .then(files => files.map(f => fs.stat(f)))
  .then(files => console.log('glob + files.map/stat', files))
  .catch(error => console.error(error))

glob + files.map/stat [ Promise { <pending> },
  Promise { <pending> },
  Promise { <pending> },
  Promise { <pending> },
  Promise { <pending> },
  Promise { <pending> } ]
```

Step 3 is to use Promise.all to wait for all these promises to resolve:

```
// ...imports and arguments as before...

glob(`${srcDir}/**/*.txt`)
  .then(files => Promise.all(files.map(f => fs.stat(f))))
  .then(files => console.log('glob + Promise.all(...)', files))
  .catch(error => console.error(error))

glob + Promise.all(...) [ Stats {
    dev: 16777220,
    mode: 33188,
    ...more information... },
    ...five more Stats objects...
]
```

In step 4, we remember that we need to keep track of the names of the files we are looking at, so we need to write our own function that returns an object with two keys (one for the filename, and one for the stats). As described in Chapter 6, the notation {a, b} produces an object {"a": a, "b": b}:

```
// ...imports and arguments as before...

const statPair = (filename) => {
  return new Promise((resolve, reject) => {
    fs.stat(filename)
      .then(stats => resolve({filename, stats}))
      .catch(error => reject(error))
  })
}

glob(`${srcDir}/**/*.txt`)
  .then(files => Promise.all(files.map(f => statPair(f))))
  .then(files => console.log('glob + Promise.all(...)', files))
  .catch(error => console.error(error))

glob + Promise.all(...) [ { filename: './common-sense.txt',
    stats:
      Stats {
        dev: 16777220,
        mode: 33188,
        ...more information... }
    },
    ...five more (filename, Stats) pairs...
]
```

Step 5 is to make sure that we're only working with files more than 100,000 characters long:

```
// ...imports and arguments as before...

glob(`${srcDir}/**/*.txt`)
  .then(files => Promise.all(files.map(f => statPair(f))))
  .then(files => files.filter(pair => pair.stats.size > 100000))
  .then(files => Promise.all(files.map(f => fs.readFile(f.filename, 'utf8'))))
  .then(contents => console.log('...readFile', contents.map(c => c.length)))
  .catch(error => console.error(error))
```

```
...readFile [ 148134, 1070331, 248369, 1276201, 706124, 204492 ]
```

In step 6, we split each file's content into lines and count:

```
// ...imports and arguments as before...

const countLines = (text) => {
  return text.split('\n').length
}

glob(`${srcDir}/**/*.txt`)
  .then(files => Promise.all(files.map(f => statPair(f))))
  .then(files => files.filter(pair => pair.stats.size > 100000))
  .then(files => Promise.all(files.map(f => fs.readFile(f.filename, 'utf8'))))
  .then(contents => contents.map(c => countLines(c)))
  .then(lengths => console.log('lengths', lengths))
  .catch(error => console.error(error))
```

```
lengths [ 2654, 21063, 4105, 22334, 13028, 3584 ]
```

There's a lot going on in the example above but the important points are:

- Promises always return another `Promise` object.
- This allows us to chain multiple `then` calls.
- This chain is formed of processes that will each wait to run until their predecessor has completed.
- A single `catch` method works to handle exceptions raised by *any* of the previous steps.

9.4   ASYNC AND AWAIT

Programmers are never content to leave well enough alone, so the latest version of JavaScript offers yet another tool for managing asynchronous computation. As we saw above, the result of `Promise.then` is another promise, which allows us to create long chains of `.then(...)` calls. It works, but it isn't the most readable of notations and has been known to create a feeling of being trapped.

We can avoid this using two new keywords, `async` and `await`. `async` tells JavaScript that a function is asynchronous, i.e., that it might want to wait for something to complete. Inside an asynchronous function, `await` tells JavaScript to act as if it had waited for something to finish. We use the two together like this:

```
const fs = require('fs-extra')

const statPairAsync = async (filename) => {
  const stats = await fs.stat(filename)
  return {filename, stats}
}

statPairAsync('moby-dick.txt').then(
  (white_whale) => console.log(white_whale.stats))
```

An `async` function still returns a `Promise`, but we can chain those promises together with other `async` functions using `await`, which collects the result returned
by a resolved promise. As before, we can use `.catch` to handle any errors thrown.

Let's use these to convert the complete example from the previous section:

```
const fs = require('fs-extra')
const glob = require('glob-promise')

const statPairAsync = async (filename) => {
  const stats = await fs.stat(filename)
  return {filename, stats}
}

const countLines = (text) => {
  return text.split('\n').length
}

const processFiles = async (globpath) => {
  const filenames = await glob(globpath)
  const pairs = await Promise.all(
    filenames.map(f => statPairAsync(f)))
  const filtered = pairs.filter(
    pair => pair.stats.size > 100000)
  const contents = await Promise.all(
    filtered.map(f => fs.readFile(f.filename, 'utf8')))
  const lengths = contents.map(c => countLines(c))
  console.log(lengths)
}

const srcDir = process.argv[2]

processFiles(`${srcDir}/**/*.txt`)
  .catch(e => console.log(e.message))
```

Using `async` and `await` lets us avoid long `then` chains; unless and until
JavaScript allows us to define operators like R's %>% pipe operator, they are probably
the easiest way to write readable code. Note, though, that we can only use `await` inside `async` functions: JavaScript will report a syntax error if we use them elsewhere.
In particular, we cannot use them interactively unless we wrap whatever we want to
do in a wee function.

9.5   EXERCISES

WHAT'S GOING ON?

This code runs fine:

```
[500, 1000].forEach(t => {
  console.log(`about to setTimeout for ${t}`)
  setTimeout(() => {console.log(`inside timer handler for ${t}`)}, 0)
})
```

but this code fails:

```
console.log('starting...')
[500, 1000].forEach(t => {
  console.log(`about to setTimeout for ${t}`)
  setTimeout(() => {console.log(`inside timer handler for ${t}`)}, 0)
})
```

Why?

A STAY OF EXECUTION

Insert a call to `console.log` in the appropriate place in the code block below so that the output reads

```
Waiting...
This is a sharp Medicine, but it is a Physician for all diseases and miseries.
Waiting...
Finished.
```

```
const holdingMessage = () => {
  console.log('Waiting...')
}

const swingAxe = () => {
  setTimeout(() => {
    holdingMessage()
    console.log('Finished.')
  }, 100)
  holdingMessage()
}

swingAxe()
```

A SYNCHRONOUS OR ASYNCHRONOUS?

Which of these functions would you expect to be asynchronous? How can you tell? Does it matter? And, if so, what is a good strategy to find out for sure if a function is asynchronous?

1. `findNearestTown(coords)`: given a set of coordinates (`coords`) in Brazil, looks up and returns the name of the nearest settlement with an estimated population greater than 5000. The function throws an error if `coords` fall outside Brazil.
2. `calculateSphereVolume(r)`: calculates and returns the volume of a sphere with radius `r`.
3. `calculateRoute(A,B)`: returns all possible routes by air between airports `A` and `B`, including direct routes and those with no more than 2 transfers.

HANDLING EXCEPTIONS

What (if any) output would you expect to see in the console when the code below is executed?

```
const checkForBlanks = (inputValue) => {
  return new Promise((resolve, reject) => {
    if (inputValue === '') {
      reject(Error("Blank values are not allowed"))
    } else {
      resolve(inputValue)
    }
  })
}

new Promise((resolve, reject) => {
  setTimeout(() => {
    reject(Error('Timed out!'))
  }, 1000)
  resolve('')
}).then(
  output => checkForBlanks(output), error => console.log(error.message)).then(
    checkedOutput => console.log(checkedOutput)).catch(
      error => console.log(error.message))
```

1. Timed out!
2. blank output
3. Blank values are not allowed
4. a new Promise object

EMPTY PROMISES

Fill in the blanks (___) in the code block below so that the function returns Array[7, 8, 2, 6, 5].

```
const makePromise = (someInteger) => {
  return ___ Promise((resolve, reject) => {
    setTimeout(___(someInteger), someInteger * 1000)
  })
}
Promise.___([makePromise(7), makePromise(___), makePromise(2),
            makePromise(6), makePromise(5)]).then(
  numbers => ___(numbers))
```

Now adapt the function so that it returns only 2. (Hint: you can achieve this by changing only one of the blank fields.)

ASYNC, THEREFORE I AM

Using async and await, convert the completed function above into an asynchronous function with the same behavior and output. Do you find your solution easier to read and follow than the original version? Do you think that that is only because you wrote this version?

KEY POINTS

- JavaScript keeps an execution queue for delayed computations.
- Use promises to manage delayed computation instead of raw callbacks.
- Use a callback with two arguments to handle successful completion (resolve) and unsuccessful completion (reject) of a promise.
- Use `then` to express the next step after successful completion and `catch` to handle errors.
- Use `Promise.all` to wait for all promises in a list to complete and `Promise.race` to wait for the first promise in a set to complete.
- Use `await` to wait for the result of a computation.
- Mark functions that can be waited on with `async`.

10 Interactive Sites

Browsers allow us to define **event handlers** to specify what to do in response to an externally-triggered action, such as a page loading or a user pressing a button. These event handlers are just callback functions that are (usually) given an **event object** containing information about what happened, and while we can write them in pure JavaScript, they're even easier to build in React.

Let's switch back to single-page examples for a moment to show how we pass a callback function as a specifically-named property of the thing whose behavior we are specifying. (Don't forget to load the required libraries in the HTML header, like we did in Chapter 7.)

```
<body>
  <div id="app"></div>
  <script type="text/babel">
    let counter = 0
    const sayHello = (event) => {
      counter += 1
      console.log(`Hello, button: ${counter}`)
    }

    ReactDOM.render(
      <button onClick={sayHello}>click this</button>,
      document.getElementById("app")
    )
  </script>
</body>
```

As its name suggests, `onClick` is the event handler called when a button is clicked. Here, we are telling React to call `sayHello`, which adds one to the event object `counter` and then prints its value along with a greeting message.

Global variables and functions are a poor way to structure code. It's far better to define the component as a class and then use a method as the event handler:

```
<body>
  <div id="app"></div>
  <script type="text/babel">
    class Counter extends React.Component {

      constructor (props) {
        super(props)
        this.state = {counter: 0}
      }

      increment = (event) => {
        this.setState({counter: this.state.counter+1})
      }
```

```
        render = () => {
          return (
            <p>
              <button onClick={this.increment}>increment</button>
              <br/>
              current: {this.state.counter}
            </p>
          )
        }
      }

      ReactDOM.render(
        <Counter />,
        document.getElementById("app")
      )
    </script>
  </body>
</html>
```

Working from bottom to top, the ReactDOM.render call inserts whatever HTML is produced by <Counter /> into the element whose ID is "app". In this case, though, the counter is not a function, but a class with three parts:

1. Its constructor passes the properties provided by the user to React.Component's constructor. (There aren't any properties in this case, but there will be in future examples, so it's a good habit to get into.) The constructor then creates a property called state that holds this component's state. This property *must* have this name so that React knows to watch it for changes.
2. The increment method uses setState (inherited from React.Component) to change the value of the counter. We *must* do this rather than creating and modifying this.counter so that React will notice the change in state and re-draw what it needs to.
3. The render method takes the place of the functions we have been using so far. It can do anything it wants, but must return some HTML (using JSX). Here, it creates a button with an event handler and displays the current value of the counter.

React calls each component's render method each time setState is used to update the component's state. Behind the scenes, React does some thinking to minimize how much redrawing takes place: while it may look as though the paragraph, button, and current count are all being redrawn each time, React will only actually redraw as little as it can.

10.1 BUT IT DOESN'T WORK

If we try running this little application from the command line with Parcel:

```
$ npm run dev -- src/interactive/display-counter.html
```

everything works as planned. But now try taking the code out of the web page and putting it in its own file:

```html
<html>
  <head>
    <meta charset="utf-8">
    <title>Counter</title>
    <script src="app.js" async></script>
  </head>
  <body>
    <div id="app"></div>
  </body>
</html>
```

```javascript
import React from 'react'
import ReactDOM from 'react-dom'

class Counter extends React.Component {

  constructor (props) {
    // ...as before...
  }

  increment = (event) => {
    this.setState({counter: this.state.counter+1})
  }

  render = () => {
    // ...as before...
  }
}

ReactDOM.render(
  <Counter />,
  document.getElementById('app')
)
```

Let's try running this:

```
$ npm run dev -- src/interactive/counter/index.html
```

```
> js4ds@0.1.0 dev /Users/stj/js4ds
> parcel serve -p 4000 "src/interactive/counter/index.html"

Server running at http://localhost:4000
!!  /Users/stj/js4ds/src/interactive/counter/app.js:11:12: \
  Unexpected token (11:12)
   9 |   }
  10 |
> 11 |   increment = (event) => {
     |             ^
  12 |     this.setState({counter: this.state.counter+1})
  13 |   }
  14 |
```

It seems that Parcel doesn't like fat arrow methods. This happens because React is still using ES6 JavaScript by default, and fat arrow methods weren't included in

JavaScript at that point. All right, let's try using "normal" function-style method definitions instead:

```
// ...imports as before...

class Counter extends React.Component {

  constructor (props) {
    super(props)
    this.state = {counter: 0}
  }

  increment (event) {
    this.setState({counter: this.state.counter+1})
  }

  render () {
    return (
      <p>
        <button onClick={this.increment}>increment</button>
        <br/>
        current: {this.state.counter}
      </p>
    )
  }
}

// ...render as before...
```

Parcel runs this without complaint, but clicking on the button doesn't change the display. Despair is once again our friend—our *only* friend—but we persevere. When we open the debugging console in the browser, we see the message `TypeError: this is undefined`. Section G.3 explains in detail why this happens; for now, suffice to say that some poor choices were made early in JavaScript's development about variable scoping.

At this point it appears that we can compile but not run, or not bundle files together. But wait—when we used an in-page script, we specified the type as `text/babel` and loaded:

```
https://unpkg.com/babel-standalone@6/babel.js
```

in the page header along with React. Can Babel save us?

The answer is "yes", though it takes a fair bit of searching on the web to find this out (particularly if you don't know what you're looking for). The magic is to create a file in the project's root directory called `.babelrc` and add the following lines:

```
{
  "presets": [
    "react"
  ],
  "plugins": [
    "transform-class-properties"
```

```
    ]
}
```

Once we've done this, we can use NPM to install `babel-preset-react` and `babel-plugin-transform-class-properties` and then switch back to fat arrow methods. Voila: everything works.

What's happening here is that when Babel translates our sparkly modern JavaScript into old-fashioned JavaScript compatible with all browsers, it reads `.babelrc` and obeys that configuration. The settings above tell it to do everything React needs using the `transform-class-properties` plugin; in particular, to accept fat arrow method definitions and bind `this` correctly. This works, but is a form of madness: something outside our program determines how that program is interpreted, and the commands controlling it go in yet another configuration file. Still, it is a useful form of madness, so we will press on.

10.2 MODELS AND VIEWS

Well-designed applications separate **models** (which store data) from **views** (which display it) so that each can be tested and modified independently. When we use React, the models are typically classes, and the views are typically pure functions.

To introduce this architecture, let's re-implement the counter using:

- `App` to store the state and provide methods for altering it,
- `NumberDisplay` to display a number, and
- `UpAndDown` to provide buttons that increment and decrement that number.

The crucial design feature is that `NumberDisplay` and `UpAndDown` don't know what they're displaying or what actions are being taken on their behalf, which makes them easier to re-use. Of course, no good deed goes unpunished. The price that we pay for organizing our application into separate components is that now we must import the dependencies of each component and export the component itself within each script.

After we've done this, our dependencies will be bundled by parcel. So we must remove the script loading from the HTML header. The whole page is:

```
<html>
  <head>
    <meta charset="utf-8">
    <title>Up and Down</title>
  </head>
  <body>
    <div id="app"></div>
    <script src="app.js"></script>
  </body>
</html>
```

The `NumberDisplay` class takes a label and a value and puts them in a paragraph (remember, the label and value will appear in our function as properties of the `props` parameter):

```
const NumberDisplay = (props) => {
  return (<p>{props.label}: {props.value}</p>)
}
```

Similarly, UpAndDown expects two functions as its up and down properties, and makes each the event handler for an appropriately-labelled button:

```
const UpAndDown = (props) => {
  return (
    <p>
      <button onClick={props.up}> [+] </button>
      <button onClick={props.down}> [-] </button>
    </p>
  )
}
```

Both of these components will use React and ReactDOM when they are rendered so we must import these. We do this by adding import statements to the beginning of both components:

```
import React from "react"
import ReactDOM from "react-dom"
```

Similarly, our application will need to import the UpAndDown and NumberDisplay components, so we need to export them after they've been defined. This is done by adding export {<object_name>} to the end of the component script. (We will explore why the curly braces are necessary in the exercises.) After we've done this for UpAndDown, the complete component script looks like this:

```
import React from "react"
import ReactDOM from "react-dom"

const UpAndDown = (props) => {
  return (
    <p>
      <button onClick={props.up}> [+] </button>
      <button onClick={props.down}> [-] </button>
    </p>
  )
}

export {UpAndDown}
```

We are now ready to build the overall application. It creates a state containing a counter and defines methods to increment or decrement the counter's value. Its render method then lays out the buttons and the current state using those elements (Figure 10.1):

```
class App extends React.Component {
```

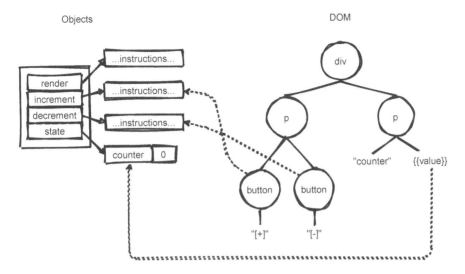

Figure 10.1: React Objects and the DOM

```
constructor (props) {
  super(props)
  this.state = {counter: 0}
}

increment = (event) => {
  this.setState({counter: this.state.counter + 1})
}

decrement = (event) => {
  this.setState({counter: this.state.counter - 1})
}

render = () => {
  return (
    <div>
      <UpAndDown up={this.increment} down={this.decrement} />
      <NumberDisplay label='counter' value={this.state.counter} />
    </div>
  )
}
}
```

We must import the dependencies as we did with the other components. As well as React and ReactDOM, we need to include the components that we've written. Dependencies stored locally can be imported by providing the path to the file in which they are defined, with the .js removed from the file name:

```
import React from "react"
import ReactDOM from "react-dom"
```

```
import {UpAndDown} from "./UpAndDown"
import {NumberDisplay} from "./NumberDisplay"

// ...script body...
```

Finally, we can render the application with `ReactDOM` as before:

```
// ...script body...

const mount = document.getElementById("app")
ReactDOM.render(<App/>, mount)
```

This seems pretty complicated because it is: our small example would be much simpler without all this indirection. However, we need this strategy to manage large applications: data and event handlers are defined in one class, then passed into display components to be displayed and interacted with.

10.3 FETCHING DATA

Let's use what we've learned to look at how the world might end. NASA provides a web interface to get information about near-approach asteroids. We will use it to build a small display with:

- a text box for submitting a starting date (get one week by default), and
- a list of asteroids in that time period.

Here's the first version of our **App** class:

```
import React from "react"
import ReactDOM from "react-dom"
import {AsteroidList} from "./AsteroidList"
import {DateSubmit} from "./DateSubmit"

class App extends React.Component {

  constructor (props) {
    super(props)
    this.state = {
      // ...fill in...
    }
  }

  onNewDate = (text) => {
    // ...fill in...
  }

  render = () => {
    return (
      <div>
        <DateSubmit newValue={this.onNewDate} />
        <AsteroidList asteroids={this.state.asteroids} />
```

```
      </div>
    )
  }
}

const mount = document.getElementById("app")
ReactDOM.render(<App/>, mount)
```

We'll test it by displaying asteroids using fake data; as in our first example, the display component AsteroidList doesn't modify data, but just displays it in a table:

```
import React from "react"
import ReactDOM from "react-dom"

const AsteroidList = (props) => {
  return (
    <table>
      <tbody>
      <tr>
        <th>Name</th>
        <th>Date</th>
        <th>Diameter (m)</th>
        <th>Approach (km)</th>
      </tr>
      {props.asteroids.map((a) => {
        return (
          <tr key={a.name}>
            <td>{a.name}</td>
            <td>{a.date}</td>
            <td>{a.diameter}</td>
            <td>{a.distance}</td>
          </tr>
        )
      })}
      </tbody>
    </table>
  )
}

export {AsteroidList}
```

React will complain if we don't provide a unique key to distinguish elements that we create, since having these keys helps it keep track of the component-to-DOM relationship, which in turn makes updates much more efficient[1]. Since each asteroid's name is supposed to be unique, we use that name as the key for each table row.

---

[1] https://stackoverflow.com/questions/28329382/understanding-unique-keys-for-array-children-in-react-js

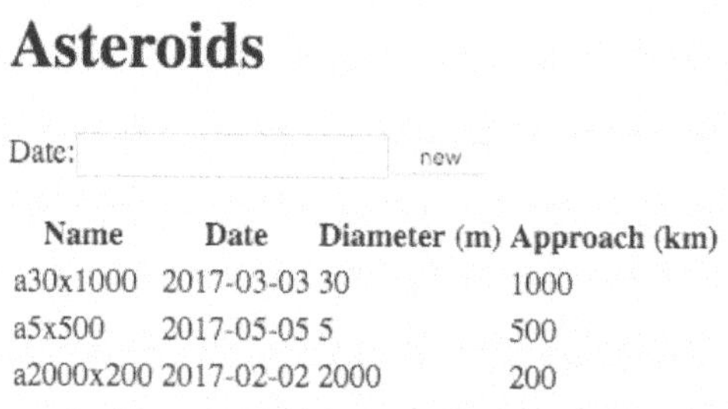

Asteroids

Date: [_____]   new

Name	Date	Diameter (m)	Approach (km)
a30x1000	2017-03-03	30	1000
a5x500	2017-05-05	5	500
a2000x200	2017-02-02	2000	200

Figure 10.2: Asteroids Application

`AsteroidList` expects data to arrive in `props.asteroids`, so let's put some made-up values in `App` for now that we can then pass in:

```
class App extends React.Component {

  constructor (props) {
    super(props)
    this.state = {
      asteroids: [
        {name: 'a30x1000', date: '2017-03-03',
         diameter: 30, distance: 1000},
        {name: 'a5x500', date: '2017-05-05',
         diameter: 5, distance: 500},
        {name: 'a2000x200', date: '2017-02-02',
         diameter: 2000, distance: 200}
      ]
    }
  }

  // ...other code...
}
```

Let's also create a placeholder for `DateSubmit`:

```
import React from "react"
import ReactDOM from "react-dom"

const DateSubmit = (props) => {
  return (<p>DateSubmit</p>)
}

export {DateSubmit}
```

and run it to get Figure 10.2.

The next step is to handle date submission. Since we're trying to instill good practices, we will make a reusable component whose caller will pass in:

• a text label;

- a variable to update with the current value of a text box;
- a function to call when the text box's value changes; and
- another function to call when a button is clicked to submit.

```
// ...imports as before...

const DateSubmit = ({label, value, onChange, onCommit}) => {
  return (
    <p>
      {label}:
      <input type="text" value={value}
             onChange={(event) => onChange(event.target.value)} />
      <button onClick={(event) => onCommit(value)}>new</button>
    </p>
  )
}

export {DateSubmit}
```

Note the use of destructuring in DateSubmit's parameter list; this was introduced in Section 6.4 and is an easy way to pull values out of the props parameter.

It's important to understand the order of operations in the example above. value={value} puts a value in the input box to display each time DateSubmit is called. We re-bind onChange and onClick to functions on each call as well (remember, JSX gets translated into function calls). So yes, this whole paragraph is being re-created every time someone types, but React and the browser work together to minimize recalculation.

Back to our application:

```
// ...imports as before...

class App extends React.Component {

  constructor (props) {
    super(props)
    this.state = {
      newDate: '',
      asteroids: [
        //...data as before...
      ]
    }
  }

  onEditNewDate = (text) => {
    this.setState({newDate: text})
  }

  onSubmitNewDate = (text) => {
    console.log(`new date ${text}`)
    this.setState({newDate: ''})
  }

  render = () => {
```

```
    return (
      <div>
        <h1>Asteroids</h1>
        <DateSubmit
          label='Date'
          value={this.state.newDate}
          onChange={this.onEditNewDate}
          onCommit={this.onSubmitNewDate} />
        <AsteroidList asteroids={this.state.asteroids} />
      </div>
    )
  }
}

// ...mount as before...
```

It's safe to pass `this.state.newDate` to `value` because we're re-drawing each
time there's a change; remember, we're passing a value for display, not a reference
to be modified. And note that we are not doing any kind of validation: the user could
type `abc123` as a date and we would blithely try to process it.

It's now time to get real data, which we will do using `fetch` with a URL. This
returns a promise (Chapter 9), so we'll handle the result of the fetch in the promise's
`then` method, and then chain another `then` method to transform the data into what
we need:

```
// ...previous code as before...

  onSubmitNewDate = (text) => {
    const url = 'https://api.nasa.gov/neo/rest/v1/feed' +
                `?api_key=DEMO_KEY&start_date=${text}`
    fetch(url).then((response) => {
      return response.json()
    }).then((raw) => {
      const asteroids = this.transform(raw)
      this.setState({
        newDate: '',
        asteroids: asteroids
      })
    })
  }

//...render as before...
```

Line by line, the steps are:

1. Build the URL for the data
2. Start to fetch data from that URL
3. Give a callback to execute when the data arrives
4. Give another callback to use when the data has been converted from text to JSON
   (which we will look at in more detail in Chapter 11).
5. Transform that data from its raw form into the objects we need

6. Set state

Finally, the method to transform the data NASA gives us is:

```
// ...previous code as before...

  transform = (raw) => {
    let result = []
    for (let key in raw.near_earth_objects) {
      raw.near_earth_objects[key].forEach((asteroid) => {
        result.push({
          name: asteroid.name,
          date: asteroid.close_approach_data[0].close_approach_date,
          diameter: asteroid.estimated_diameter.meters.estimated_diameter_max,
          distance: asteroid.close_approach_data[0].miss_distance.kilometers
        })
      })
    }
    return result
  }

// ...render as before...
```

We built this by looking at the structure of the JSON that NASA returned and figuring out how to index the fields we need. (Unfortunately, the top level of near_earth_objects is an object with dates as keys rather than an array, so we have to use let... in... rather than purely map or forEach.)

10.4 EXERCISES

RESET

Add a "reset" button to the counter application that always sets the counter's value to zero. Does using it to wipe out every change you've made to the counter feel like a metaphor for programming in general?

TRANSFORM

Modify all of the examples *after* the introduction of Babel to use external scripts rather than in-pace scripts.

EXPORTS

Are the curly braces necessary when exporting from a component file? What happens if you remove them? Read this blogpost[2] and then consider whether it might have been more appropriate to use default exports and imports in the examples above.

---

[2]http://2ality.com/2014/09/es6-modules-final.html

VALIDATION

Modify the application so that if the starting date isn't valid when the button is clicked, the application displays a warning message instead of fetching data.

1. Add a field called `validDate` to the state and initialize it to `true`.
2. Add an `ErrorMessage` component that displays a paragraph containing either "date OK" or "date invalid" depending on the value of `validDate`.
3. Modify `onSubmitNewDate` so that it *either* fetches new data *or* modifies `validDate`.

Once you are done, search the Internet for React validation and error messages and explore other tools you could use to do this.

KEY POINTS

- Define event handlers to specify what actions the browser should take when the user interacts with an application.
- The browser passes event objects containing details of events to event handlers.
- Use classes to keep state and event handlers together.
- React calls a class's `render` to display it.
- Separate models (which store data) from views (which display it).
- Use `fetch` to get data from servers.
- Use destructuring to get individual members from an object in a single step.
- Modern JavaScript uses promises to manage asynchronous activities.

11 Managing Data

There's not much point creating interactive web pages if they don't have something to interact with. To provide that, we need something to store data and something to serve it. We could build one program to do both, but experience teaches that it's better to create one for each so that they are easier to understand, test, and maintain. After tossing a coin, we decide to start with the data store; Chapter 12 will look at how to build a server.

11.1 DATA FORMATS

The most widely used text format for tabular data is undoubtedly **comma-separated values** (CSV). Each row of the table is a line in the file; the values within each row—i.e., the columns—are separated by commas. Numbers appear as themselves; strings may or may not be wrapped in quotation marks, unless they contain commas themselves, in which case they definitely are:

```
"maroon",128,0,0
"olive",128,128,0
"aqua",0,255,255
"fuchsia",255,0,255
```

The first line of a CSV file is often a **header row** that defines the names of the columns. For example, the small table shown above would better be represented as:

```
"name","red","green","blue"
"maroon",128,0,0
"olive",128,128,0
"aqua",0,255,255
"fuchsia",255,0,255
```

Tragically, CSV doesn't require the first row to be a header, and CSV files usually don't specify units or data types. We can guess that the values in the table above are integers, but it's all too common to have a CSV file whose columns are labelled "height" and "weight" without any indication of whether the heights are in feet or meters or the weights in pounds or kilograms.

CSV is good for tabular data, but a lot of data doesn't neatly fit into rows and columns. Many programmers use **JSON** instead: it supports a subset of the syntax for values, arrays, and objects in JavaScript, so that (for example) we can store configuration values for a program like this:

```
{
  "name" : "DataExplorer",
  "version" : "1.2.1",
  "preferences" : {
```

```
    "colorscheme" : "dark",
    "autofill" : true
  },
  "last_opened" : [
    "raw/biotic.dat",
    "raw/genomic.dat",
    "cooked/inferred.dat"
  ]
}
```

JSON can be used for tabular data as well. The whole table is an array, and each record is an object with name-value pairs:

```
const colors = [
  {"name": "maroon", "red": 128, "green": 0, "blue": 0},
  {"name": "olive", "red": 128, "green": 128, "blue": 0},
  {"name": "aqua", "red": 0, "green": 255, "blue": 255},
  {"name": "fuchsia", "red": 255, "green": 0, "blue": 255}
]
```

Repeating field names like this is wasteful compared to listing them once at the top of a table, but it does mean that the fields within rows can be accessed directly using expressions like colors[1].red.

11.2   SLICING DATA

The data we will use as an example is available in a variety of formats from the Portal Project Teaching Database[1]. We will focus on surveys.csv, which has over 35,500 records. That's a lot to look at, so we will create a 10-record slice for testing.

Although it would be easy to take the first ten, or the last, there's a good chance that neither would be representative of the data as a whole. Instead, we will write a little script that selects some records at random. Since it doesn't need to be efficient, we will read everything, pair each line with a random number, sort the lines using those random numbers as keys, then take the top few lines.

```
const fs = require('fs')

const [inputFile, numLines, outputFile] = process.argv.splice(2)
const lines = fs.readFileSync(inputFile, 'utf-8')
      .split('\n')
header = lines[0]
const sample = lines.slice(1)
      .map(line => [Math.random(), line])
      .sort((left, right) => { return left[0] - right[0] })
      .slice(0, parseInt(numLines))
      .map(pair => pair[1])
fs.writeFileSync(outputFile, header + '\n' + sample.join('\n'))
```

---

[1]https://figshare.com/articles/Portal_Project_Teaching_Database/1314459

When we run this on the command line:

```
$ node select-random.js ../../data/surveys.csv 10 slice.csv
```

we get:

```
record_id,month,day,year,plot_id,species_id,sex,hindfoot_length,weight
18501,3,14,1991,13,OT,M,21,28
2283,1,15,1980,11,OL,M,21,23
19941,5,2,1992,1,PP,M,22,13
27413,12,29,1997,5,,,,
16002,5,9,1989,19,SC,,,
28813,11,21,1998,12,DO,M,35,56
9338,7,4,1984,11,DO,F,35,57
28336,8,22,1998,7,PB,M,26,23
25323,3,16,1997,9,DM,F,33,26
6785,10,23,1982,5,DM,F,37,45
```

Running it again will probably generate a different data slice, since we're not specifying a random number generation **seed**. We are bad people, and will fix this in the exercises.

Slicing Command-Line Arguments

When we run:
```
$ node select-random.js ../../data/surveys.csv 10 slice.csv
```
 the array `process.argv` *contains five strings: the* `node` *command, the name of our script* `select-random.js`*, and then the name of the input file, the number of lines we can, and the name of the output file.* `process.argv.slice(2)` *discards elements 0 and 1 from this list, leaving us the three values we need to assign to* `inputFile`*,* `numLines`*, and* `outputFile` *respectively. We will explore a better way to do this in the exercises.*

11.3 DATA MANAGER

Rather arbitrarily, we decide that our data manager will be able to answer two questions:

1. How many records do we have and what range of years do they cover? This is the kind of opening question that many client programs will ask.
2. What are the minimum, average, and maximum values for weight and hindfoot length by year for a given range of years? This would be very specific to a particular kind of client program; a good service would either provide many such specialized queries or provide a way to apply common **aggregation functions** to particular columns.

We will use PapaParse[2] to parse our CSV, so our first step is to install it:

---
[2]https://www.papaparse.com/

```
$ npm install papaparse
```

After loading the library and reading our test data file a couple of times, we break down and read the documentation, then come up with this as the first version of our data manager:

```javascript
const fs = require('fs')
const papa = require('papaparse')

class DataManager {

  constructor (filename) {
    const raw = fs.readFileSync(filename, 'utf-8')
    const options = {header: true, dynamicTyping: true}
    this.data = papa.parse(raw, options).data
  }
}

module.exports = DataManager
```

`papa.parse` takes two arguments: the CSV file to be parsed and a configuration object that controls how the parser behaves. This configuration object is highly customizable.; here, our `options` instruct the parser to interpret the first row as a header (which sets column names) and to convert things that look like numbers to numbers (the `dynamicTyping` option). The output of `papa.parse` looks like this:

```
{ data:
   [ { record_id: 18501,
       month: 3,
       day: 14,
       year: 1991,
       plot_id: 13,
       species_id: 'OT',
       sex: 'M',
       hindfoot_length: 21,
       weight: 28 },

     ...eight more records...

     { record_id: 6785,
       month: 10,
       day: 23,
       year: 1982,
       plot_id: 5,
       species_id: 'DM',
       sex: 'F',
       hindfoot_length: 37,
       weight: 45 } ],
  errors: [],
  meta:
   { delimiter: ',',
     linebreak: '\n',
     aborted: false,
```

```
      truncated: false,
      cursor: 350,
      fields:
       [ 'record_id',
         'month',
         'day',
         'year',
         'plot_id',
         'species_id',
         'sex',
         'hindfoot_length',
         'weight' ] } }
```

so `papa.parse(raw, options).data` gets the data we want as JSON. Let's write
a method to get some overall statistics:

```
getSurveyStats () {
  return {
    year_low : this._get(this.data, 'year', Math.min),
    year_high : this._get(this.data, 'year', Math.max),
    record_count : this.data.length
  }
}

// ...other methods...

_get(values, field, func) {
  return func(...values.map(rec => rec[field]).filter(val => !isNaN(val)))
}
```

Functions like `Math.min` and `Math.max` take any number of scalar values as
arguments, but do not directly process arrays. Enter **spread syntax** `...`: the notation `func(...array)` means "pass all the values in the array as separate arguments", which saves us from writing our own minimum and maximum functions.
Thus, `func(...this.data.map(rec => rec[field]))` means "select the specified field from each record in `this.data` to create an array of fields, then pass all
of those values as arguments to `func`. We include an underscore at the start of the
name of `_get` to indicate that we intend it to be used only inside `DataManager` and
not to be called elsewhere.

Adding the method to get weight and hindfoot length for a range of years is comparatively straightforward. First, we write a function to calculate the average of one
or more arguments:

```
const _average = (...values) => {
  let sum = 0
  for (let v of values) {
    sum += v
  }
  return sum / values.length
}
```

It would be more natural for `_average` to take an array rather than a variable number of arguments, but we want to be able to use it in the same way that we use `Math.min` and `Math.max`, so we have to conform to their signature.

After some thought we realize that it's possible for `subset` to be empty—i.e., it's possible that there are years that have no data in our dataset. We should filter these out, to prevent unnecessary effort being made to render summary statistics with `NaN` values. Remembering that empty arrays are not falsy in JavaScript (Chapter 2), we decide to test that the `subset` returned by filtering for each year contains at least one entry.

The last thing that we need to ensure is that each data object has a unique key, which will make it much easier for React to efficiently update the display of the data when we are ready to render it.

The method to get the values for a range of years is now:

```
getSurveyRange (minYear, maxYear) {
  return Array(1 + maxYear - minYear)
    .fill(0)
    .map((v, i) => minYear + i)
    .map(year => {
      const subset = this.data.filter(r => r.year === year)
      if (subset.length) {
        return {
          key  : toString(year),
          year : year,
          min_hindfoot_length :this._get(subset,
                                 'hindfoot_length', Math.min),
          ave_hindfoot_length : this._get(subset,
                                  'hindfoot_length', _average),
          max_hindfoot_length : this._get(subset,
                                  'hindfoot_length', Math.max),
          min_weight : this._get(subset, 'weight', Math.min),
          ave_weight : this._get(subset, 'weight', _average),
          max_weight : this._get(subset, 'weight', Math.max)
        }
      }
    }
  })
}
```

11.4 EXERCISES

TRACING DATA

Trace the execution of the utility program that creates a small sample of the original data, explaining what is passed into each of the chained methods calls.

UNRANDOM

Programs that rely on random numbers are impossible to test because there's (deliberately) no way to predict their output. Luckily, computer programs don't actually use random numbers: they use **pseudo-random numbers** that are generated in a repeatable but unpredictable way. Given the same initial **seed**, a pseudo-random number generator will always produce the same sequence of values.

There is no way to set a seed for `Math.random` out of the box, but the seedrandom[3] package provides an add-on function for this purpose. Install the package and modify the slice selection utility so that it takes a word or phrase as a command-line argument and uses it to seed the random number generator.

ONE RECORD PER YEAR

Another way to slice the data for testing purposes is to select one record from each year. Write a small command-line JavaScript program that:

1. Reads all the data from the CSV.
2. Keeps the first record it finds for each year.
3. Prints these records formatted as SQL `insert` statements.

ERROR HANDLING

Modify `DataManager`'s constructor so that it checks for errors.

GENERALIZATION

Modify `getSurveyRange` so that it can be called like this:

```
getSurveyRange(minYear, maxYear, 'hindfoot_length', 'weight')
```

i.e., so that the names of the fields whose minimum, average, and maximum values are wanted can be passed as strings, and the method will automatically create the right names and values in its result.

HANDLING COMMAND-LINE ARGUMENTS

Read the documentation for the `command-line-args`[4] package and rewrite the data slicing script to use it instead of `process.argv.slice`.

KEY POINTS

- Small tabular datasets are commonly stored as Comma-Separated Values (CSV).
- CSV can only represent regular data, and CSV files usually don't include units.
- Nested data is commonly stored using JavaScript Object Notation (JSON).
- JSON representations of tabular data often include redundant (and therefore possibly inconsistent) specifications of column names.
- PapaParse is a robust CSV parsing library that produces JSON output.

---

[3]https://www.npmjs.com/package/seedrandom

[4]https://www.npmjs.com/package/command-line-args

12 Creating a Server

Now that we have a data manager (Chapter 11) the next step is to create a server to share our data with the world, which we will build using a library called Express[1]. Before we start writing code, though, we need to understand how computers talk to each other.

12.1 HTTP

Almost everything on the web communicates via the HyperText Transfer Protocol (**HTTP**). The core of HTTP is a **request/response** cycle that specifies the kinds of requests applications can make of servers, how they exchange data, and so on. Figure 12.1 shows this cycle in action for a page that includes one image.

1. The client (a browser or some other program) makes a connection to a server.
2. It then sends a blob of text specifying what it's asking for.
3. The server replies with a blob of text and the HTML.
4. The connection is closed.
5. The client parses the text and realizes it needs an image.
6. It sends another blob of text to the server asking for that image.
7. The server replies with a blob of text and the contents of the image file.
8. The connection is closed.

This cycle might be repeated many times to display a single web page, since a separate request has to be made for every image, every CSS or JavaScript file, and so on. In practice, a lot of behind-the-scenes engineering is done to keep connections alive as long as they're needed, and to **cache** items that are likely to be re-used.

An HTTP request is just a block of text with two important parts:

- The **method** is almost always either GET (to get data) or POST (to submit data).
- The **URL** is typically a path to a file, but as we'll see below, it's completely up to the server to interpret it.

---

[1]https://expressjs.com/

Figure 12.1: HTTP Request/Response Cycle

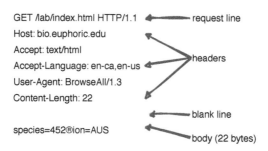

Figure 12.2: Structure of an HTTP Request

The request can also contain **headers**, which are key-value pairs with more information about what the client wants. Some examples include:

- "`Accept: text/html`" to specify that the client wants HTML
- "`Accept-Language: fr, en`" to specify that the client prefers French, but will accept English
- "`If-Modified-Since: 16-May-2018`" to tell the server that the client is only interested in recent data

Unlike a dictionary, a key may appear any number of times, which allows a request to do things like specify that it's willing to accept several types of content. The **body** of the request is any extra data associated with it, such as files that are being uploaded. If a body is present, the request must contain the `Content-Length` header so that the server knows how much data to read (Figure 12.2).

The headers and body in an HTTP response have the same form, and mean the same thing. Crucially, the response also includes a **status code** to indicate what happened: 200 for OK, 404 for "page not found", and so on. Some of the more common are shown in Table 12.1.

One final thing we need to understand is the structure and interpretation of URLs. This one:

`http://example.org:1234/some/path?value=deferred&limit=200`

has five parts:

- The protocol `http`, which specifies what rules are going to be used to exchange data.
- The **hostname** `example.org`, which tells the client where to find the server. If we are running a server on our own computer for testing, we can use the name `localhost` to connect to it. (Computers rely on a service called **DNS** to find the machines associated with human-readable hostnames, but its operation is out of scope for this tutorial.)

Code	Name	Meaning
100	Continue	The client should continue sending data
200	OK	The request has succeeded
204	No Content	The server completed the request but there is no data
301	Moved Permanently	The resource has moved to a new permanent location
307	Temporary Redirect	The resource is temporarily at a different location
400	Bad Request	The request is badly formatted
401	Unauthorized	The request requires authentication
404	Not Found	The requested resource could not be found
408	Timeout	The server gave up waiting for the client
418	I'm a Teapot	An April Fool's joke
500	Internal Server Error	A server error occurred while handling the request
601	Connection Timed Out	The server did not respond before the connection timed out

Table 12.1
HTTP Status Codes

- The **port** 1234, which tells the client where to call the service it wants. (If a host is like an office building, a port is like a phone number in that building. The fact that we think of phone numbers as having physical locations says something about our age...)
- The path /some/path tells the server what the client wants.
- The **query parameters** value=deferred and limit=200. These come after a question mark and are separated by ampersands, and are used to provide extra information.

It used to be common for paths to identify actual files on the server, but the server can interpret the path however it wants. In particular, when we are writing a data service, the segments of the path can identify what data we are asking for. Alternatively, it's common to think of the path as identifying a function on the server that we want to call, and to think of the query parameters as the arguments to that function. We'll return to these ideas after we've seen how a simple server works.

12.2 HELLO, EXPRESS

A Node-based library called Express handles most of the details of HTTP for us. When we build a server using Express, we provide callback functions that take three parameters:

- the original request,
- the response we're building up, and
- what to do next (which we'll ignore for now).

We also provide a pattern with each function that specifies what URLs it is to match. Here is a simple example:

```
const express = require('express')

const PORT = 3418

// Main server object.
const app = express()

// Return a static page.
app.get('/', (req, res, next) => {
  res.status(200).send('<html><body><h1>Asteroids</h1></body></html>')
})

app.listen(PORT, () => { console.log('listening...') })
```

The first line of code loads the Express library. The next defines the port we will listen on, and then the third creates the object that will do most of the work.

Further down, the call to `app.get` tells that object to handle any GET request for '/' by sending a reply whose status is 200 (OK) and whose body is an HTML page containing only an h1 heading. There is no actual HTML file on disk, and in fact no way for the browser to know if there was one or not: the server can send whatever it wants in response to whatever requests it wants to handle.

Note that `app.get` doesn't actually get anything right away. Instead, it registers a callback with Express that says, "When you see this URL, call this function to handle it." As we'll see below, we can register as many path/callback pairs as we want to handle different things.

Finally, the last line of this script tells our application to listen on the specified port, while the callback tells it to print a message as it starts running. When we run this, we see:

```
$ node static-page.js

listening...
```

Our little server is now waiting for something to ask it for something. If we go to our browser and request `http://localhost:3418/`, we get a page with a large title `Asteroids` on it. Our server has worked, and we can now stop it by typing Ctrl-C in the shell.

12.3   HANDLING MULTIPLE PATHS

Let's extend our server to do different things when given different paths, and to handle the case where the request path is not known:

```
const express = require('express')

const PORT = 3418

// Main server object.
const app = express()
```

```
// Root page.
app.get('/', (req, res, next) => {
  res.status(200).send('<html><body><h1>Home</h1></body></html>')
})

// Alternative page.
app.get('/asteroids', (req, res, next) => {
  res.status(200).send('<html><body><h1>Asteroids</h1></body></html>')
})

// Nothing else worked.
app.use((req, res, next) => {
  res
    .status(404)
    .send(`<html><body><p>ERROR: ${req.url} not found</p></body></html>`)
})

app.listen(PORT, () => { console.log('listening...') })
```

The first few lines are the same as before. We then specify handlers for the paths / and /asteroids, each of which sends a different chunk of HTML.

The call to app.use specifies a default handler: if none of the app.get handlers above it took care of the request, this callback function will send a "page not found" code *and* a page containing an error message. Some sites skip the first part and only return error messages in pages for people to read, but this is sinful: making the code explicit makes it a lot easier to write programs to scrape data.

As before, we can run our server from the command line and then go to various URLs to test it. http://localhost:3418/ produces a page with the title "Home", http://localhost:3418/asteroids produces one with the title "Asteroids", and http://localhost:3418/test produces an error page.

12.4 SERVING FILES FROM DISK

It's common to generate HTML in memory when building data services, but it's also common for the server to return files. To do this, we will provide our server with the path to the directory it's allowed to read pages from, and then run it with node server-name.js path/to/directory. We have to tell the server whence it's allowed to read files because we definitely do *not* want it to be able to send everything on our computer to whoever asks for it. (For example, a request for the /etc/passwd password file on a Linux server should probably be refused.)

Here's our updated server:

```
const express = require('express')
const path = require('path')
const fs = require('fs')

const PORT = 3418
const root = process.argv[2]
```

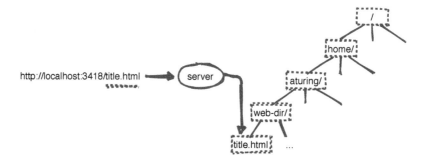

Figure 12.3: Mapping URLs to Files

```
// Main server object.
const app = express()

// Handle all requests.
app.use((req, res, next) => {
  const actual = path.join(root, req.url)
  const data = fs.readFileSync(actual, 'utf-8')
  res.status(200).send(data)
})

app.listen(PORT, () => { console.log('listening...') })
```

The steps in handling a request are:

1. The URL requested by the client is given to us in `req.url`.
2. We use `path.join` to combine that with the path to the root directory, which we got from a command-line argument when the server was run.
3. We try to read that file using `readFileSync`, which blocks the server until the file is read. We will see later how to do this I/O asynchronously so that our server is more responsive.
4. Once the file has been read, we return it with a status code of 200.

If a sub-directory called `web-dir` holds a file called `title.html`, and we run the server as:

```
$ node serve-pages.js ./web-dir
```

we can then ask for `http://localhost:3418/title.html` and get the content of `web-dir/title.html`. Notice that the directory `./web-dir` doesn't appear in the URL: our server interprets all paths as if the directory we've given it is the root of the filesystem.

If we ask for a nonexistent page like `http://localhost:3418/missing.html` we get this:

```
Error: ENOENT: no such file or directory, open 'web-dir/missing.html'
    at Object.openSync (fs.js:434:3)
    at Object.readFileSync (fs.js:339:35)
    ... etc. ...
```

We will see in the exercises how to add proper error handling to our server.

Favorites and Icons

If we use a browser to request a page such as title.html, *the browser may actually make two requests: one for the page, and one for a file called* favicon.ico. *Browsers do this automatically, then display that file in tabs, bookmark lists, and so on. Despite its* .ico *suffix, the file is (usually) a small PNG-formatted image, and must be placed in the root directory of the website.*

12.5   CONTENT TYPES

So far we have only served HTML, but the server can send any type of data, including images and other binary files. For example, let's serve some JSON data:

```
// ...as before...

app.use((req, res, next) => {
  const actual = path.join(root, req.url)

  if (actual.endsWith('.json')) {
    const data = fs.readFileSync(actual, 'utf-8')
    const json = JSON.parse(data)
    res.setHeader('Content-Type', 'application/json')
    res.status(200).send(json)
  }

  else {
    const data = fs.readFileSync(actual, 'utf-8')
    res.status(200).send(data)
  }
})
```

What's different here is that when the requested path ends with .json we explicitly set the Content-Type header to application/json to tell the client how to interpret the bytes we're sending back. If we run this server with web-dir as the directory to serve from and ask for http://localhost:3418/data.json, a modern browser will provide a folding display of the data rather than displaying the raw text.

So What's an API?

A library's **Application Programming Interface** *(API) is simply the set of functions other programs are allowed to call. This is usually a subset of all of the functions defined in the library, since many may be helpers intended for internal use only. Similarly, a server's API is the set of requests it knows how to respond to. For example, NASA's near-approach asteroid API (Section 10.3) can handle requests that include an authentication* *key and a starting date, while the server we have built in this chapter can respond to requests for HTML and JSON files. We will look a little more closely at API design in Section 15.2.*

12.6 EXERCISES

REPORT MISSING FILES

Modify the version of the server that returns files from disk to report a 404 error if a file cannot be found. What should it return if the file exists but cannot be read (e.g., if the server does not have permissions)?

SERVING IMAGES

Modify the version of the server that returns files from disk so that if the file it is asked for has a name ending in `.png` or `.jpg`, it is returned with the right `Content-Type` header.

DELAYED REPLIES

Our file server uses `fs.readFileSync` to read files, which means that it stops each time a file is requested rather than handling other queries while waiting for the file to be read. Modify the callback given to `app.use` so that it uses `fs.readFile` with a callback instead.

USING QUERY PARAMETERS

URLs can contain query parameters in the form:

```
http://site.edu?first=123&second=beta
```

Read the online documentation for Express[2] to find out how to access them in a server, and then write a server to do simple arithmetic: the URL `http://localhost:3654/add?left=1&right=2` should return 3, while the URL `http://localhost:3654/subtract?left=1&right=2` should return -1.

KEY POINTS

- An HTTP request or response consists of a plain-text header and an optional body.
- HTTP is a stateless protocol.
- Express provides a simple path-based JavaScript server.
- Write callback functions to handle requests matching specified paths.
- Provide a default handler for unrecognized requests.
- Use `Content-Type` to specify the type of data being returned.
- Use dynamic loading to support plugin extensions.

---

[2]https://expressjs.com/

13 Testing

We are bad people, because we have been writing code without testing it. In this lesson we will redeem ourselves (partially) by correcting that (also partially).

JavaScript uses the same pattern for **unit testing** as most other modern languages. Each test is written as a function, and each of those functions tests one particular aspect of the code. A standalone program called a **test runner** finds test functions, runs them, and reports the results. Any setup code that needs to be run before each test to create the data for the test's input (called its **fixture**) is put in a function of its own. Similarly (but less frequently), if some teardown needs to be done *after* each test, we put those operations in a function as well.

Each unit test can have one of three results:

- pass: everything worked,
- fail: the system being tested didn't do what was expected, or
- error: something went wrong with the test itself.

We can combine tests into **test suites** (and test suites into larger suites, and so on) so that we can more easily run related sets of tests. This makes testing during development faster, which in turn makes it more likely that we'll actually do it. Finally, we write the tests themselves using **assertions**: statements that check whether or not some condition holds and generate an error if it doesn't. Node provides an `assert` library with some useful functions for asserting various things; we'll explore this as we go along.

13.1 INTRODUCING MOCHA

JavaScript has almost as many testing libraries as it has front-end frameworks. We will use one called Mocha[1] that is popular and well documented. Unlike the libraries we have seen before, we don't import anything to use it; instead, *it* imports *our* code and calls our functions.

When we're writing tests for Mocha to run, we use a function called `describe` to create a group of tests and another function called `it` for each test in that group:

```
describe('first test', () => {
  it('should run without errors', (done) => {
    done()
  })
})
```

---

[1] https://mochajs.org/

As this example shows, `describe`'s arguments are an explanatory string and a callback function. That callback makes calls to `it`, which takes:

- another explanatory string describing how the system should behave, and
- a callback that receives a function (called done by convention).

(The name `it` was chosen so that when we read tests aloud, it sounds like we're saying, "It should do this or that.") At the end of each test we call done to signal that it has finished. We have to do this because callbacks run out of order, so Mocha needs to know when each one completes.

We can run our tests from the shell by invoking `mocha` and giving it the path to the file that contains the tests:

```
$ ./node_modules/.bin/mocha path/to/test.js


  first test
    + should run without errors


  1 passing (12ms)
```

As with bundling, we normally put the `mocha` command in `package.json` so that `./node_modules/.bin` is automatically included in the path. After we add this:

```
{
  ...
  "scripts": {
    ...
    "test": "mocha",
    ...
  }
}
```

to `package.json`, our command becomes:

```
$ npm test -- path/to/test.js
```

(Again, everything after `--` is passed to the script itself.) If we don't specify where to find tests, Mocha looks for a directory called `test` and runs the files it finds there whose names begin with `test` (Figure 13.1).

13.2 REFACTORING

The next step is to **refactor** our software to make it testable. In the case of our server, we have to:

- move the code that listens on a port into one file, and
- have that import a file that contains the code to do everything else.

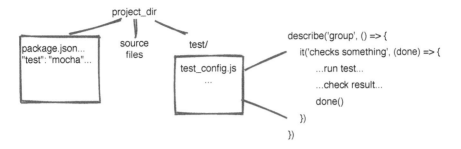

Figure 13.1: Mocha in Action

Once we have done this, we can run the server code in other contexts. Here's the file `standalone.js` that actually launches a server:

```
const server = require('./server')
const PORT = 3418
server.listen(PORT,
              () => { console.log(`listening on port ${PORT}...`) })
```

And here is the application code we've extracted into `server.js` so that we can test it:

```
const express = require('express')

// Main server object.
let app = express()

// Root page.
app.get('/', (req, res, next) => {
  res.status(200).send('<html><body><h1>Home</h1></body></html>')
})

// ...as before...

module.exports = app
```

Before going any further, we check that we haven't broken anything by running:

```
$ node standalone.js
```

13.3 TESTING THE SERVER

All right: now that we have extracted the code that's specific to our server, how do we test it? The answer is yet another library called supertest[2] that sends fake HTTP requests to an Express server that has been split in the way we just split ours and lets us interact with that server's replies.

---

[2]https://github.com/visionmedia/supertest

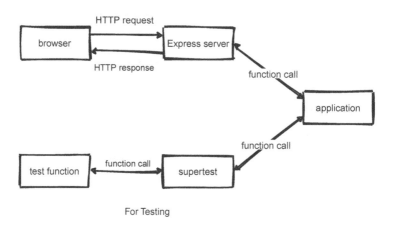

Figure 13.2: Supertest versus Reality

Here's a test of a simple request that uses Mocha to manage the test, and supertest's `request` function to send something to the server and check the result:

```
const assert = require('assert')
const request = require('supertest')
const server = require('./server')

describe('server', () => {

  it('should return HTML with expected title', (done) => {
    request(server)
      .get('/')
      .expect(200)
      .expect('Content-Type', /html/)
      .end((err, res) => {
        assert(res.text.includes('Home'), 'Has expected title')
        done()
      })
  })
})
```

Going through this line by line:

1. `request(server)` starts building up a request to send.
2. `.get('/')` specifies the path in the URL we are sending.
3. `.expect(200)` checks that the return code is 200 (OK).
4. `.expect('Content-Type', /html/)` checks the content type in the returned value against a **regular expression** (Appendix H).
5. `.end` is called when the whole response has been received, i.e., when we can start looking at the content of the page or data that the server has sent.

6. Inside the callback to end, res is the result data. We make sure that its text (i.e., res.text) includes the word "Home". We really should check err here to make sure everything worked properly, but we're not quite that virtuous.
7. Finally, we call done() to signal the end of the test. Again, we have to do this because there's no way Mocha can know when the enclosing .end(...) will be called

Let's run our code:

```
server
  + should return HTML with expected title (48ms)


1 passing (58ms)
```

Excellent: let's add some more tests.

```
describe('server', () => {

  it('should return HTML with expected title', (done) => {
    // ...as before...
  })

  it('should return page as HTML with expected title', (done) => {
    request(server)
      .get('/asteroids')
      .expect(200)
      .expect('Content-Type', /html/)
      .end((err, res) => {
        assert(res.text.includes('Asteroids'), 'Has expected title')
        done()
      })
  })

  it('should 404 for other pages', (done) => {
    request(server)
      .expect(404)
      .get('/other')
      .end((err, res) => {
        assert(res.text.includes('ERROR'), 'Has expected error message')
        done()
      })
  })
})
```

```
server
  + should return HTML with expected title (42ms)
  + should return asteroids page as HTML with expected title
  + should 404 for other pages


3 passing (62ms)
```

Notice that we check to make sure that the server sends a 404 when we ask for something that doesn't exist. Making sure the system fails gracefully is just as important as making sure that it provides data when asked to.

13.4   CHECKING THE HTML

It's increasingly common for servers to return data that is rendered by the client rather than generating and returning HTML, but some servers still do the latter. Do *not* try to check this with substrings or regular expressions: the exceptions have exceptions, and that way lies madness[3]. Instead, we should parse the HTML to create a structure in memory and check that; if parsing fails because the HTML is badly formatted, that's worth knowing too. The structure in question is our new friend the DOM, and to get it, we will use (yet another) library called cheerio[4]. cheerio.load turns HTML text into a DOM tree; the resulting object can be used like a function, and we can use the same selectors we met previously to find things in it. Here's our test:

```
const assert = require('assert')
const request = require('supertest')
const cheerio = require('cheerio')
const server = require('./server')

describe('server', () => {
  it('should have the correct headings', (done) => {
    request(server)
      .get('/')
      .expect('Content-Type', /html/)
      .expect(200)
      .end((err, res) => {
        const tree = cheerio.load(res.text)
        assert.equal(tree('h1').length, 1, 'Correct number of headings')
        assert.equal(tree('h1').text(), 'Home', 'Correct heading text')
        done()
      })
  })
})
```

```
  server
    + should have the correct headings (67ms)


  1 passing (77ms)
```

This gets the page as before, parses it, then looks for h1 elements and checks the text of the first one. (Note that this *doesn't* check if the title is Home because .text() concatenates all the text of the children.) We won't explore this approach further because we're going to serve data for rendering rather than generating HTML and sending that, but if you're doing any web scraping at all, libraries like cheerio are there to help.

---

[3]https://stackoverflow.com/a/1732454

[4]https://cheerio.js.org/

13.5 EXERCISES

NOT DONE

What happens if we forget to call done() in a test?

ADDING TESTS

1. What is the most useful test you could add for the asteroids application? Why?
2. Implement it.
3. Ask yourself why tutorials like this one don't say "*please* implement it". Reflect on the fact that this question didn't say "please" either. Are you comfortable with the paternalistic power relationship embodied in the absence of that one little word, and with the somewhat uncomfortable attempt at ironic humor embodied in this question?

LIFECYCLE

Suppose a JavaScript program contains some JSX expressions that produce HTML which is then read and displayed by a browser. Draw a diagram to show the form taken by an H1 heading containing the word "data" from start to finish.

KEY POINTS

- A unit test checks the behavior of one software component in isolation.
- The result of a unit test can be pass, fail, or error.
- Use Mocha to write and run unit tests in JavaScript.
- Put assertions in unit tests to check results.
- Combine tests in suites for easier management.
- Divide modules into interactive and non-interactive parts for easier testing.
- Use supertest to simulate interaction with a server for testing.
- HTML is represented in memory using the Document Object Model (DOM).
- Check the structure of the DOM rather than the textual representation of the HTML when testing.

14 Using Data-Forge

We have now seen how to do everything a data scientist would want to do in JavaScript except actual data science. This is unfortunately one of the areas where the language still lags behind R and Python, but statistical libraries are now appearing, and if the last twenty-five years have taught us anything, it's not to underestimate JavaScript.

In this chapter we will look at a library called Data-Forge that is designed for working with tabular data. Data-Forge was inspired by Python's Pandas library, but should be familiar to anyone who has worked with the tidyverse in R as well. Its **DataFrame** class represents a table made up of named columns and any number of rows. Dataframes are **immutable**: once a dataframe has been constructed, its contents cannot be changed. Instead, every operation produces a new dataframe. (Some clever behind-the-scenes data recycling makes this much more efficient than it sounds.)

Like Pandas and the tidyverse, Data-Forge is designed to work on **tidy data**. As defined in [Wick2014], tabular data is tidy if:

- Each column contains one statistical variable (i.e., one property that was measured or observed).
- Each different observation is in a different row.
- There is one table for each set of observations.
- If there are multiple tables, each table has a column containing a unique key so that related data can be linked.

For example, this data is not tidy:

Rodent Pleurisy Rates				
	Female		Male	
	2018	2019	2018	2019
Jan	0.05	0.07	0.03	0.06
Feb	0.05	0.08	0.04	0.07
Mar	0.05	0.11	0.04	0.10

but this data is:

Year	Month	Sex	Rate
2018	Jan	Female	0.05
2018	Feb	Female	0.05
2018	Mar	Female	0.05
2018	Jan	Male	0.03
2018	Feb	Male	0.04

2018	Mar	Male	0.04
2019	Jan	Female	0.07
2019	Feb	Female	0.08
2019	Mar	Female	0.11
2019	Jan	Male	0.06
2019	Feb	Male	0.07
2019	Mar	Male	0.10

14.1 BASIC OPERATIONS

To get started, we install Data-Forge using `npm install data-forge` and then load the library and create a dataframe from a list of objects. Each of these objects must use the same keys, which become the names of the dataframe's columns:

```
const DF = require('data-forge')

const fromObjects = new DF.DataFrame([
    {ones: 1, tens: 10},
    {ones: 2, tens: 20},
    {ones: 3, tens: 30}
])
console.log('fromObjects:\n', fromObjects)
```

When we print the dataframe, we see this rather complex structure:

```
fromObjects:
 DataFrame {
  configFn: null,
  content:
   { index: CountIterable {},
     values: [ [Object], [Object], [Object] ],
     pairs: MultiIterable { iterables: [Array] },
     isBaked: true,
     columnNames: [ 'ones', 'tens' ] } }
```

Each column is stored as a `Series` object; once in a while, we will need to work with these objects directly instead of with the dataframe as a whole. (Figure 14.1). If we want to see the actual data, we need to convert the dataframe back to an array of objects:

```
console.log('fromObjects as array:\n', fromObjects.toArray())
```

```
fromObjects as array:
 [ { ones: 1, tens: 10 },
   { ones: 2, tens: 20 },
   { ones: 3, tens: 30 } ]
```

We can instead create a dataframe by providing the names of the columns in one list and the rows' values in another:

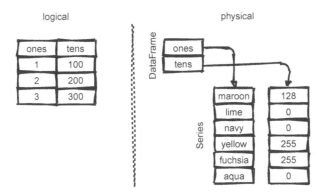

Figure 14.1: How Tables Are Stored

```
const fromSpec = new DF.DataFrame({
  columnNames: ['ones', 'tens'],
  rows: [
    [4, 40],
    [5, 50],
    [6, 60]
  ]
})
console.log('fromSpec as array:\n', fromSpec.toArray())


fromSpec as array:
 [ { ones: 4, tens: 40 },
   { ones: 5, tens: 50 },
   { ones: 6, tens: 60 } ]
```

However, we usually won't create a dataframe directly like this; instead, we will read data from a file or a database. Data-Forge provides a function called fromCSV for doing this:

```
const text = `ones,tens
7,70
8,80
9,90`
const fromText = DF.fromCSV(text)
console.log('fromText as array:\n', fromText.toArray())


fromText as array:
 [ { ones: '7', tens: '70' },
   { ones: '8', tens: '80' },
   { ones: '9', tens: '90' } ]
```

However we create our dataframe, we can ask it for its columns' names:

```
console.log(data.getColumnNames())
```

```
[ 'ones', 'tens' ]
```

or get its content as a list of lists (rather than as a list of objects):

```
console.log(data.toRows())
```

```
[ [ 1, 10 ], [ 2, 20 ], [ 3, 30 ] ]
```

We can also process the rows using a for loop:

```
for (let row of data) {
  console.log(row)
}
```

```
{ ones: 1, tens: 10 }
{ ones: 2, tens: 20 }
{ ones: 3, tens: 30 }
```

or its forEach method:

```
data.forEach(row => {
  console.log(row)
})
```

```
{ ones: 1, tens: 10 }
{ ones: 2, tens: 20 }
{ ones: 3, tens: 30 }
```

However, a good rule of thumb is that if you're using a loop on a dataframe, you're doing the wrong thing: you should instead use the methods described below.

14.2 DOING CALCULATIONS

Suppose we want to add a new column to a dataframe—or rather, create a new dataframe with an extra column, since we can't modify a dataframe in place. To do this, we create a new Series object to represent that column, then use withSeries to construct our result:

```
const double_oh = new DF.Series([100, 200, 300])
```

```
const withHundreds = data.withSeries({hundreds: double_oh})
console.log(withHundreds.toArray())
```

```
[ { ones: 1, tens: 10, hundreds: 100 },
  { ones: 2, tens: 20, hundreds: 200 },
  { ones: 3, tens: 30, hundreds: 300 } ]
```

Just as we usually create dataframes by reading data from external sources, we will usually create new columns from existing values. As you probably won't be surprised to learn, we tell Data-Forge how to do this by writing callback functions. Since we often want to create several new columns at once, we give the generateSeries method an object whose keys are the names of the new columns and whose values are callbacks taking a row as input and producing a new value as output:

```
const sumsAndProducts = data.generateSeries({
  sum: row => row.ones + row.tens,
  product: row => row.ones * row.tens
})
console.log(sumsAndProducts.toArray())
```

```
[ { ones: 1, tens: 10, sum: 11, product: 10 },
  { ones: 2, tens: 20, sum: 22, product: 40 },
  { ones: 3, tens: 30, sum: 33, product: 90 } ]
```

We can also get rid of columns entirely using dropSeries:

```
const justResults = sumsAndProducts.dropSeries(["ones", "tens"])
console.log(justResults.toArray())
```

```
[ { sum: 11, product: 10 },
  { sum: 22, product: 40 },
  { sum: 33, product: 90 } ]
```

Since every dataframe method returns a dataframe, we can use **method chaining** to combine operations (Figure 14.2). We have seen this technique before with chains of .then calls on promises; here, it is used like pipes in the Unix command line or the pipe operator %>% in modern R code:

```
const result = data
  .withSeries({hundreds: double_oh})
  .generateSeries({
    sum: row => row.ones + row.tens + row.hundreds
  })
  .dropSeries(["ones", "tens", "hundreds"])
  .toArray()
```

To make results easier to understand, we will often want to sort our data. Suppose we have a file containing the red-green-blue values for several colors:

```
name,red,green,blue
maroon,128,0,0
lime,0,255,0
navy,0,0,128
yellow,255,255,0
fuchsia,255,0,255
aqua,0,255,255
```

We can pass the name of this file to our program as a command-line argument, read it (remembering to set the encoding to UTF-8 so that we get characters rather than raw bytes), and then display it:

```
const fs = require('fs')
const DF = require('data-forge')

const text = fs.readFileSync(process.argv[2], 'utf-8')
const colors = DF.fromCSV(text)
console.log(colors.toArray())
```

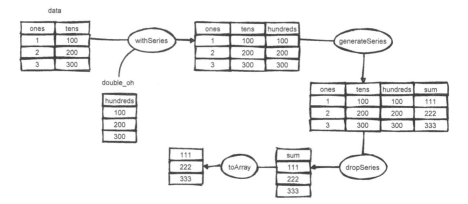

Figure 14.2: A More Complicated Pipeline

```
[ { name: 'maroon', red: '128', green: '0', blue: '0' },
  { name: 'lime', red: '0', green: '255', blue: '0' },
  { name: 'navy', red: '0', green: '0', blue: '128' },
  { name: 'yellow', red: '255', green: '255', blue: '0' },
  { name: 'fuchsia', red: '255', green: '0', blue: '255' },
  { name: 'aqua', red: '0', green: '255', blue: '255' } ]
```

If we want to see the colors in alphabetical order, we call `orderBy` with a callback that gives Data-Forge the value to sort by:

```
const sorted = colors.orderBy(row => row.name)
console.log(sorted.toArray())
```

```
[ { name: 'aqua', red: '0', green: '255', blue: '255' },
  { name: 'fuchsia', red: '255', green: '0', blue: '255' },
  { name: 'lime', red: '0', green: '255', blue: '0' },
  { name: 'maroon', red: '128', green: '0', blue: '0' },
  { name: 'navy', red: '0', green: '0', blue: '128' },
  { name: 'yellow', red: '255', green: '255', blue: '0' } ]
```

To sub-sort (Figure 14.3) by another column we use `thenBy`:

```
const doubleSorted = colors
      .orderBy(row => row.green)
      .thenBy(row => row.blue)
      .dropSeries(['name', 'red'])
console.log(doubleSorted.toArray())
```

```
[ { green: '0', blue: '0' },
  { green: '0', blue: '128' },
  { green: '0', blue: '255' },
```

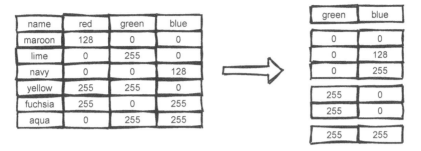

Figure 14.3: Sorting and Sub-sorting

```
{ green: '255', blue: '0' },
{ green: '255', blue: '0' },
{ green: '255', blue: '255' } ]
```

We can remove duplicates with `distinct`:

```
const notTheSame = colors.distinct(row => row.red)
console.log(notTheSame.toArray())
```

```
[ { name: 'maroon', red: '128', green: '0', blue: '0' },
  { name: 'lime', red: '0', green: '255', blue: '0' },
  { name: 'yellow', red: '255', green: '255', blue: '0' } ]
```

but this is trickier than it appears. Each row does indeed have a distinct red value, but Data-Forge gets to decide which row to keep from each subset. What's more surprising is that multi-column `distinct` *doesn't* work:

```
const multiColumn = colors
      .distinct(row => [row.red, row.green])
      .orderBy(row => row.red)
      .thenBy(row => row.green)
console.log(multiColumn.toArray())
```

```
[ { name: 'navy', red: '0', green: '0', blue: '128' },
  { name: 'lime', red: '0', green: '255', blue: '0' },
  { name: 'aqua', red: '0', green: '255', blue: '255' },
  { name: 'maroon', red: '128', green: '0', blue: '0' },
  { name: 'fuchsia', red: '255', green: '0', blue: '255' },
  { name: 'yellow', red: '255', green: '255', blue: '0' } ]
```

This isn't Data-Forge's fault. In JavaScript, two arrays are only equal if they're the same object, i.e., `[0]` `===` `[0]` is `false`. We will explore ways of doing multi-column `distinct` in the exercises.

14.3 SUBSETS

You may have noticed that the color values in the table above are strings rather than
numbers. If we want Data-Forge to convert values to more useful types, we can use
the methods `parseDates`, `parseFloats`, and so on. The program below does this
for a subset of USGS data about earthquakes in August 2016[1]:

```
const fs = require('fs')
const DF = require('data-forge')

const text = fs.readFileSync('earthquakes.csv', 'utf-8')
const earthquakes = DF
    .fromCSV(text)
    .parseDates('Time')
    .parseFloats(['Latitude', 'Longitude', 'Depth_Km', 'Magnitude'])
console.log('Data has', earthquakes.count(), 'rows')
```

```
Data has 798 rows
```

Whether we convert it or not, we will often want to work with subsets of data. We
can select values by position using `head` and `tail` (which are named after classic
Unix commands):

```
console.log(earthquakes.head(3).toArray())
```

```
[ { Time: 2016-08-24T07:36:32.000Z,
    Latitude: 42.6983,
    Longitude: 13.2335,
    Depth_Km: 8.1,
    Magnitude: 6 },
  { Time: 2016-08-24T07:37:26.580Z,
    Latitude: 42.7123,
    Longitude: 13.2533,
    Depth_Km: 9,
    Magnitude: 4.5 },
  { Time: 2016-08-24T07:40:46.590Z,
    Latitude: 42.7647,
    Longitude: 13.1723,
    Depth_Km: 9.7,
    Magnitude: 3.8 } ]
```

```
console.log(earthquakes.tail(3).toArray())
```

```
[ { Time: 2016-08-26T10:09:45.380Z,
    Latitude: 42.6953,
    Longitude: 13.2363,
    Depth_Km: 9.5,
    Magnitude: 2.3 },
  { Time: 2016-08-26T10:11:55.960Z,
    Latitude: 42.6163,
```

---

[1]https://earthquake.usgs.gov/earthquakes/feed/v1.0/csv.php

```
       Longitude: 13.2985,
       Depth_Km: 11,
       Magnitude: 2.1 },
     { Time: 2016-08-26T10:21:09.870Z,
       Latitude: 42.6153,
       Longitude: 13.2952,
       Depth_Km: 7.5,
       Magnitude: 3 } ]
```

If we want data from the middle of the table, we can skip a few rows and then take as many as we want (Figure 14.4):

```
console.log(earthquakes.skip(10).take(3).toArray())
```

```
[ { Time: 2016-08-24T07:47:51.540Z,
    Latitude: 42.6675,
    Longitude: 13.3238,
    Depth_Km: 6.5,
    Magnitude: 3.3 },
  { Time: 2016-08-24T07:52:25.710Z,
    Latitude: 42.7447,
    Longitude: 13.2827,
    Depth_Km: 7.9,
    Magnitude: 2.9 },
  { Time: 2016-08-24T07:52:43.210Z,
    Latitude: 42.6378,
    Longitude: 13.2313,
    Depth_Km: 10.9,
    Magnitude: 3.1 } ]
```

However, it's far more common to select rows by the values they contain rather than by their position. Just like the `Array.filter` method we met way back in Section 3.4, we do this by giving Data-Forge a callback function that tells it whether a given row should be kept or not. This text can be as complex as desired, but must work row by row: we cannot make a decision about one row based on the values in the rows before it or after it.

```
const large = earthquakes.where(row => (row.Magnitude >= 5.0))
console.log(large.toArray())
```

```
[ { Time: 2016-08-24T07:36:32.000Z,
    Latitude: 42.6983,
    Longitude: 13.2335,
    Depth_Km: 8.1,
    Magnitude: 6 },
  { Time: 2016-08-24T08:33:28.890Z,
    Latitude: 42.7922,
    Longitude: 13.1507,
    Depth_Km: 8,
    Magnitude: 5.4 } ]
```

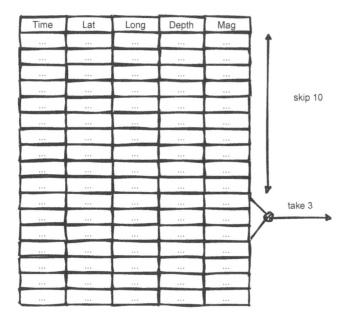

Figure 14.4: Selecting by Position

14.4   AGGREGATION

Working with individual observations is all very well, but if we want to understand our data, we need to look at its aggregate properties. If, for example, we want to know the average depth and magnitude of our earthquakes, we use the `summarize` method:

```
const averageValues = earthquakes.summarize({
  Depth_Km: series => series.average(),
  Magnitude: series => series.average()
})
console.log(averageValues)

{ Depth_Km: 9.545614035087722, Magnitude: 2.5397243107769376 }
```

As with `filter`, we can do many calculations at once by giving `summarize` several callbacks. The keys of the object we pass in specify the columns we want to aggregate; the callbacks invoke methods of the `Series` class that Data-Forge uses to store individual columns. Instead of producing a dataframe with a single row, `summarize` produces an object whose keys match the names of the columns in our original dataframe.

Aggregation is often combined with grouping: for example, we may want to calculate the average weight of rats of different breeds or the distribution of votes by province. The first step is to group the data:

```
const groupedByMagnitude = earthquakes.groupBy(row => row.Magnitude)
console.log(`${groupedByMagnitude.count()} groups`)
console.log(groupedByMagnitude.head(2).toArray())

28 groups
[ DataFrame {
    configFn: null,
    content:
     { index: [ExtractElementIterable],
       values: [ExtractElementIterable],
       pairs: [Array],
       isBaked: false,
       columnNames: [ColumnNamesIterable] } },
  DataFrame {
    configFn: null,
    content:
     { index: [ExtractElementIterable],
       values: [ExtractElementIterable],
       pairs: [Array],
       isBaked: false,
       columnNames: [ColumnNamesIterable] } } ]
```

As the output shows, `groupBy` returns an array containing one new dataframe for each group in our original data. Here's how we find the average depth of earthquakes according to magnitude:

```
const averaged = earthquakes
      .groupBy(row => row.Magnitude)
      .select(group => ({
        Magnitude: group.first().Magnitude,
        Depth_Km: group.deflate(row => row.Depth_Km).average()
      }))
      .inflate()
      .orderBy(row => row.Magnitude)
console.log(averaged.toArray())

[ { Magnitude: 2, Depth_Km: 9.901052631578946 },
  { Magnitude: 2.1, Depth_Km: 9.702083333333333 },
  { Magnitude: 2.2, Depth_Km: 9.843037974683545 },
  ...
  { Magnitude: 4.5, Depth_Km: 9.4 },
  { Magnitude: 5.4, Depth_Km: 8 },
  { Magnitude: 6, Depth_Km: 8.1 } ]
```

Going through this step by step:

1. The `groupBy` call produces a list of 28 dataframes, one for each distinct value of `Magnitude`.
2. `select` then converts each of these dataframes into an object whose `Magnitude` is equal to the magnitude of the group's first element and whose `Depth_Km` is the average of the depths.
   - We can use the magnitude of the group's first element because all of the magnitudes in the group are the same.

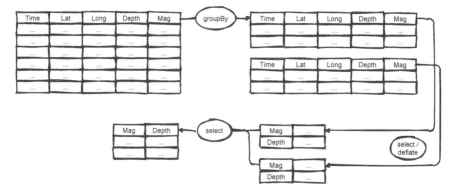

Figure 14.5: Summarizing Groups

- We must also remember to use `deflate` to turn a column of a dataframe into a `Series` so that we can then call `average`.

3. The output of `select` is a `Series` of two-valued objects, so we must call `inflate` to convert it back to a `DataFrame`.

4. Finally, we order by the magnitude of the earthquakes to produce our output.

Figure 14.5 shows these steps graphically. It's easy to forget the `inflate` and `deflate` steps at first (we did when writing this example), but they quickly become habitual.

14.5   IN REAL LIFE

To wrap up our exploration of Data-Forge, we will explore data from http://dataisplural/data.world to find the annual recreational visits to national parks in the United States for the last ten years. Our strategy is to:

1. import the data,
2. inspect the columns to make sure the data is clean,
3. fix any problems we notice,
4. group the data by year and summarize the total visitors, and then
5. filter to keep only the years that are greater than 2009.

We'll start by reading the data and looking at the first couple of rows:

```
const fs = require('fs')
const DF = require('data-forge')

const text = fs.readFileSync('../../data/national_parks.csv', 'utf-8')
const raw = DF.fromCSV(text)
console.log(raw.head(2).toArray())
```

```
[ { year: '1904',
    gnis_id: '1163670',
    geometry: 'POLYGON',
    metadata: 'NA',
    number_of_records: '1',
    parkname: 'Crater Lake',
    region: 'PW',
    state: 'OR',
    unit_code: 'CRLA',
    unit_name: 'Crater Lake National Park',
    unit_type: 'National Park',
    visitors: '1500' },
  { year: '1941',
    gnis_id: '1531834',
    geometry: 'MULTIPOLYGON',
    metadata: 'NA',
    number_of_records: '1',
    parkname: 'Lake Roosevelt',
    region: 'PW',
    state: 'WA',
    unit_code: 'LARO',
    unit_name: 'Lake Roosevelt National Recreation Area',
    unit_type: 'National Recreation Area',
    visitors: '0' } ]
```

It's always good to look at the structure of the data before we dive into any analysis. The dataframe method `detectTypes` shows us the frequency of data types in our dataframe:

```
const typesDf = raw.detectTypes()
console.log(typesDf.toString())
```

```
__index__   Type     Frequency   Column
---------   ------   ---------   -----------------
0           string   100         year
1           string   100         gnis_id
2           string   100         geometry
3           string   100         metadata
4           string   100         number_of_records
5           string   100         parkname
6           string   100         region
7           string   100         state
8           string   100         unit_code
9           string   100         unit_name
10          string   100         unit_type
11          string   100         visitors
```

We want numbers instead of strings for `year` and `visitors`, but before we transform them, let's check and see if any values in those columns are NA, meaning "not available":

```
const cleaned = raw
      .where(row => ((row.year != 'NA') && (row.visitors != 'NA')))
console.log(`${raw.count()} original rows and ${cleaned.count()} cleaned rows`)
```

```
21560 original rows and 21556 cleaned rows
```

Four rows contain missing values. We probably wouldn't spot them if we scrolled through the data ourselves, so it's good that we let the computer do the work. Let's remove those four rows and convert the two columns of interest from strings to numbers:

```
const data = raw
      .where(row => ((row.year != 'NA') && (row.visitors != 'NA')))
      .parseFloats(['year', 'visitors'])
console.log(`${data.count()} rows`)
console.log(data.detectTypes().toString())

21556 rows
__index__  Type     Frequency  Column
---------  ------   ---------  -----------------
0          number   100        year
...        ...      ...        ...
11         number   100        visitors
```

This looks good: we have dropped the four offending rows and everything else is a number. With clean data, we can now group by year and find the total number of visitors in each year:

```
const annual = data
      .groupBy(row => row.year)
      .select(group => ({
        year: group.first().year,
        visitors: group.deflate(row => row.visitors).sum()
      }))
      .inflate()
      .orderBy(row => row.year)
console.log(annual.toString())

__index__  year  visitors
---------  ----  -----------
0          1904  120690
112        1905  140954
88         NaN   13764633135
55         1906  30569
113        1907  32935
61         1908  42768
111        1909  60899
110        1910  173416
...        ...   ...
23         2011  276799292
91         2012  281392715
70         2013  271305455
89         2014  290105230
78         2015  304730566
75         2016  328483428
```

Uh oh. What's that NaN doing there in the third row? Are there still some missing values in the year column?

```
const numNan = data
    .where(row => (isNaN(row.year) || isNaN(row.visitors)))
    .count()
console.log(`${numNan} rows have NaN`)
```

```
382 rows have NaN
```

The exercises will look at where these non-numbers have come from and how we should handle them. Even if you don't live close to a national park, we encourage you to take a break and step outside before tackling the exercises below.

14.6   EXERCISES

OTHER DATA FORMATS

Write a short program that reads data from colors.csv, converts the red-green-blue values to numbers, and saves the result as JSON. Once that is working, write another program that reads the JSON file and converts it back to CSV. Are there any differences between your second program's output and your original CSV file?

DIRECTIONAL SORTING

Modify the program in Section 14.2 to sort color values by *increasing* red and *decreasing* green.

MULTI-COLUMN DISTINCT

Section 14.2 pointed out that we cannot use distinct to find rows with distinct combinations of values. What *can* we do? To show that your idea works, write a program that gets distinct combinations of red and green values from the color data:

```
red,green
0,0
0,255
128,0
255,0
255,255
```

REVISITING DATA MANIPULATION

Back in the chapter on data manipulation, we aggregated surveys.csv to find the minimum, maximum, and average values for year, hindfoot_length, and weight. Repeat this exercise using the methods of data-forge.

GROUPING AND AGGREGATING

Retrace the steps in the example that calculated the average depth of earthquakes of different magnitudes and show the data structure after each method call. Are they all dataframes, or are other data structures created or manipulated as well?

NOT A NUMBER

Write a short pipeline that prints out the values in the `year` and `visitors` columns that wind up being converted to NaN. (Hint: copy the columns, convert the copies to numbers, filter to keep those rows, then print the original values.)

KEY POINTS

- Create a `DataFrame` from an array of objects with identical keys, from a spec with `columnNames` and `rows` fields, or by parsing text that contains CSV or JSON.
- If you're using a loop on a dataframe, you're doing the wrong thing.
- Use method chaining to create pipelines that filter data and create new values from old.
- Use grouping and aggregation to summarize data.

15 Capstone Project

It's time to bring everything together in an extended example: a (slightly) interactive visualization of species data from the Portal Project Teaching Database[1]. Our plan is to:

- slice data for testing,
- write a data server to serve that data,
- test the server,
- build an interactive tabular display of our data, and
- add visualization.

This will require a few new ideas, but will mostly recapitulate what's come before.

15.1 DATA MANAGER

We could use exactly the same data manager as the one we built in Chapter 11, but let's apply our new-found knowledge of the Data-Forge library instead. As a reminder, the key class in our data manager is:

```
class DataManager {

  constructor (filename) {
    // ...read and store data from CSV file...
  }

  getSurveyStats () {
    // ...return summary statistics...
  }

  getSurveyRange (minYear, maxYear) {
    // ...return slice of data...
  }
}
```

The new `DataManager` must still begin by reading data from a CSV file, so we keep the line where we use `fs` to open the file and convert the rest of `constructor`:

```
constructor (filename) {
  const raw = fs.readFileSync(filename, 'utf-8')
  this.data = DF.fromCSV(raw)
  .parseInts(['record_id','month','day','year','plot_id'])
  .parseFloats(['hindfoot_length','weight'])
}
```

---

[1] https://figshare.com/articles/Portal_Project_Teaching_Database/1314459

Remember that _get method we had to write to summarize the data for each year? Working with dataframes allows us to avoid doing that ourselves in getSurveyStats and makes things comparatively easy to read:

```
getSurveyStats () {
  return {
    year_low: this.data.deflate(row => row.year).min(),
    year_high: this.data.deflate(row => row.year).max(),
    record_count: this.data.count()
  }
}
```

We must also adapt getSurveyRange to work with the dataframe:

```
getSurveyRange (minYear, maxYear) {
  return Array(1 + maxYear - minYear)
    .fill(0)
    .map((v, i) => minYear + i)
    .map(year => {
    const subset = this.data.where(r => r.year === year)
    if (subset.count()) {
      return {
        key: toString(year),
        year: year,
        min_hindfoot_length: subset.deflate(r => r.hindfoot_length)
                                   .min(),
        ave_hindfoot_length: subset.deflate(r => r.hindfoot_length)
                                   .average(),
        max_hindfoot_length: subset.deflate(r => r.hindfoot_length)
                                   .max(),
        min_weight: subset.deflate(r => r.weight)
                          .min(),
        ave_weight: subset.deflate(r => r.weight)
                          .average(),
        max_weight: subset.deflate(r => r.weight)
                          .max()
      }
    }
  })
}
```

This removes the need for the _get method, but when we test the code we find that blank spaces are displayed where the summary values should be for a suspicious number of years. On closer inspection, we discover that min and other summarizing methods are sensitive to missing data: they return NaN if any values are absent in the series on which they are called, or undefined if they're all missing. We therefore need an additional filter step to remove the rows with missing data in the columns that we're interested in (weight and hindfoot length):

```
// ...as before...
    if (subset.count()) {
      return {
        key: toString(year),
```

```
          year: year,
          min_hindfoot_length: subset
                               .where(r => !isNaN(r.hindfoot_length))
                               .deflate(r => r.hindfoot_length)
                               .min(),
          ave_hindfoot_length: subset
                               .where(r => !isNaN(r.hindfoot_length))
                               .deflate(r => r.hindfoot_length)
                               .average(),
          max_hindfoot_length: subset
                               .where(r => !isNaN(r.hindfoot_length))
                               .deflate(r => r.hindfoot_length)
                               .max(),
          min_weight: subset
                      .where(r => !isNaN(r.weight))
                      .deflate(r => r.weight)
                      .min(),
          ave_weight: subset
                      .where(r => !isNaN(r.weight))
                      .deflate(r => r.weight)
                      .average(),
          max_weight: subset
                      .where(r => !isNaN(r.weight))
                      .deflate(r => r.weight)
                      .max()
      }
    }
// ...as before...
```

Making these changes we discover that, although the summarizing functions run
and return NaN or undefined when presented with a series with at least one missing
observation, they throw an error when called on a completely empty series (that is,
a series of length zero). To make our data manager robust to this, we go back to
writing internal methods to ensure that data is only summarized if it actually exists
in the first place:

```
getSurveyRange (minYear, maxYear) {
  return Array(1 + maxYear - minYear)
    .fill(0)
    .map((v, i) => minYear + i)
    .map(year => {
  const subset = this.data.where(row => row.year === year)
  if (subset.count()) {
    return {
      key: toString(year),
      year: year,
      min_hindfoot_length: this._getMin(subset, 'hindfoot_length'),
      ave_hindfoot_length: this._getAve(subset, 'hindfoot_length'),
      max_hindfoot_length: this._getMax(subset, 'hindfoot_length'),
      min_weight: this._getMin(subset, 'weight'),
      ave_weight: this._getAve(subset, 'weight'),
      max_weight: this._getMax(subset, 'weight')
    }
  }
```

```
    })
  }

  _getMin (yearData, columnName) {
    const filtered = yearData.where(row => !isNaN(row[columnName]))
    if (filtered.count()) {
      return filtered.deflate(row => row[columnName]).min()
    } else {
      return 'no data'
    }
  }

  _getAve (yearData, columnName) {
    const filtered = yearData.where(row => !isNaN(row[columnName]))
    if (filtered.count()) {
      return filtered.deflate(row => row[columnName]).average()
    } else {
      return 'no data'
    }
  }

  _getMax (yearData, columnName) {
    const filtered = yearData.where(row => !isNaN(row[columnName]))
    if (filtered.count()) {
      return filtered.deflate(row => row[columnName]).max()
    } else {
      return 'no data'
    }
  }
```

15.2   SERVER

The server is going to be almost the same as the one in Chapter 12. However, we need to connect it to the data manager. We'll do this by having the driver create a data manager and then pass that data manager to the server when the latter is created:

```
const DataManager = require('./data-manager')
const server = require('./server-0')

const PORT = 3418

const filename = process.argv[2]
const db = new DataManager(filename)
const app = server(db)
app.listen(PORT, () => {
  console.log(`listening on port ${PORT}...`)
})
```

As you can probably guess from the fact that we're referring to server-0, we're going to be making some changes down the road. Here's the start of the server it works with:

```
const express = require('express')
```

```
// 'dataManager' is a global variable that refers to our database.
// It must be set when the server is created.
let dataManager = null

// Main server object.
const app = express()

// ...handle requests...

module.exports = (dbm) => {
  dataManager = dbm
  return app
}
```

We'll look at handling requests for data in the next section. The most important thing for now is the way we manage the connection to the data manager. Down at the bottom of `server-0.js`, we export a function that assigns its single argument to a variable called `dataManager`. Inside the methods that handle requests, we'll be able to send database queries to `dataManager`.

This variable is global within this file, but since it's not exported, it's invisible outside. Variables like this are called **module variables**, and give us a way to share information among the functions in a module without giving anything outside the module a way to cause (direct) harm to that information.

15.3 API

The next step is to decide what our server's API will be, i.e., what URLs it will understand and what data they will fetch. GET `/survey/stats` will get summary statistics as a single JSON record, and GET `/survey/:start/:end` gets aggregate values for a range of years. (We will add error checking on the year range as an exercise.) Anything else will return a 404 error code and a snippet of HTML telling us we're bad people. We will put this code in `server.js` and a command-line driver in `driver.js` for testability. The server functions are:

```
// Get survey statistics.
app.get('/survey/stats', (req, res, next) => {
  const data = dataManager.getSurveyStats()
  res.setHeader('Content-Type', 'application/json')
  res.status(200).send(data)
})

// Get a slice of the survey data.
app.get('/survey/:start/:end', (req, res, next) => {
  const start = parseInt(req.params.start)
  const end = parseInt(req.params.end)
  const data = dataManager.getSurveyRange(start, end)
  res.setHeader('Content-Type', 'application/json')
  res.status(200).send(data)
})
```

We also write an error handling function:

```
// Nothing else worked.
app.use((req, res, next) => {
  page = `<html><body><p>error: "${req.url}" not found</p></body></html>`
  res.status(404)
     .send(page)
})
```

Now let's write our first test:

```
const path = require('path')
const assert = require('assert')
const request = require('supertest')
const DataManager = require('./data-manager')
const make_server = require('./server-0')

TEST_DATA_PATH = path.resolve(__dirname, 'test-data.csv')

describe('server', () => {

  it('should return statistics about survey data', (done) => {
    expected = {
      minYear: 1979,
      maxYear: 2000,
      count: 10
    }
    const db = new DataManager(TEST_DATA_PATH)
    const server = make_server(db)
      .get('/survey/stats')
      .expect(200)
      .expect('Content-Type', 'application/json')
      .end((err, res) => {
        assert.deepEqual(res.body, expected, '')
        done()
      })
  })
})
```

Note that the range of years is 1979-2000, which is *not* the range in the full dataset. We run this with:

```
$ npm test -- src/capstone/back/test-server.js
```

and it passes.

15.4   THE DISPLAY

The front end is a straightforward recapitulation of what we've done before. There is a single HTML page called index.html:

```
<!DOCTYPE html>
<html>
  <head>
    <title>Creatures</title>
```

```
    <meta charset="utf-8">
    <script src="app.js" async></script>
  </head>
  <body>
    <div id="app"></div>
  </body>
</html>
```

The main application in `app.js` imports components to display summary statistics, choose a range of years, and display annual data. There is not usually such a close coupling between API calls and components, but it's not a bad place to start. Note that we are using `import` because we're trying to be modern, even though the back end still needs `require`.

```
import React from 'react'
import ReactDOM from 'react-dom'
import SurveyStats from './SurveyStats'
import ChooseRange from './ChooseRange'
import DataDisplay from './DataDisplay'

class App extends React.Component {

  constructor (props) {
    // ...constructor...
  }

  componentDidMount = () => {
    // ...initialize...
  }

  onStart = (start) => {
    // ...update start year...
  }

  onEnd = (end) => {
    // ...update end year...
  }

  onNewRange = () => {
    // ...handle submission of year range...
  }

  render = () => {
    // ...render current application state...
  }
}

ReactDOM.render(
  <App />,
  document.getElementById('app')
)
```

The constructor defines the URL for the data source and sets up the initial state, which has summary data, start and end years, and data for those years:

```
constructor (props) {
  super(props)
  this.baseUrl = 'http://localhost:3418'
  this.state = {
    summary: null,
    start: '',
    end: '',
    data: null
  }
}
```

The method `componentDidMount` is new: it fetches data for the very first time so that the user sees something useful on the page when they first load it.

```
componentDidMount = () => {
  const url = `${this.baseUrl}/survey/stats`
  fetch(url).then((response) => {
    return response.json()
  }).then((summary) => {
    this.setState({
      summary: summary
    })
  })
}
```

We don't call this method ourselves; instead, React automatically calls it once our application and its children have been loaded and initialized. We can't fetch the initial data in the application's constructor because we have no control over the order in which bits of display are initialized. On the upside, we can use `response.json()` directly because we know the source is returning JSON data. This method is the only place where the summary is updated, since the data isn't changing underneath us.

Next up we need to handle typing in the "start" and "end" boxes. The HTML controls in the web page will capture the characters without our help, but we need those values in our state variables:

```
onStart = (start) => {
  this.setState({
    start: start
  })
}

onEnd = (end) => {
  this.setState({
    end: end
  })
}
```

When the button is clicked, we send a request for JSON data to the appropriate URL and record the result in the application's state. React will notice the state change and call `render` for us. More precisely, the browser will call the first `then` callback when the response arrives, and the second `then` callback when the data has been converted to JSON.

```
onNewRange = () => {
  const params = {
    method: 'GET',
    headers: {
      'Accept': 'application/json',
      'Content-Type': 'application/json'
    }
  }
  const url = `${this.baseUrl}/survey/${this.state.start}/${this.state.end}`
  fetch(url, params).then((response) => {
    return response.json()
  }).then((data) => {
    this.setState({
      data: data
    })
  })
}
```

Now let's update the display with SurveyStats, ChooseRange, DataChart, and DataDisplay, which are all stateless components (i.e., they display things but don't change anything):

```
render = () => {
  const tableStyle = {overflow: 'scroll', height: '200px'}
  return (
    <div>
      <h1>Creatures</h1>
      <SurveyStats data={this.state.summary} />
      <ChooseRange
        start={this.state.start} onStart={this.onStart}
        end={this.state.end} onEnd={this.onEnd}
        onNewRange={this.onNewRange} />
      <DataChart data={this.state.data} />
      <div style={tableStyle}>
        <DataDisplay data={this.state.data} />
      </div>
    </div>
  )
}
```

15.5   THE TABLES

We will display survey statistics as tables, with a paragraph fallback when there's no data. First, we display summary statistics for the whole dataset (as returned by the GET /survey/stats query we wrote a handler for earlier) as a table at the top of the page. (Again, we need parentheses around the HTML fragment so that it will parse properly.)

```
import React from 'react'

const SurveyStats = ({data}) => {
  if (data === null) {
    return (<p>no data</p>)
```

```
    }
    return (
      <table>
        <tbody>
          <tr><th>record count</th><td>{data.record_count}</td></tr>
          <tr><th>year low</th><td>{data.year_low}</td></tr>
          <tr><th>year high</th><td>{data.year_high}</td></tr>
        </tbody>
      </table>
    )
}

export default SurveyStats
```

Next, we display aggregated statistics for a given range of years (the GET /survey/:start/:end query) in another table.

```
import React from 'react'

const DataDisplay = ({data}) => {

  if (! data) {
    return (<p>no data</p>)
  }

  const columns = [
    'year',
    'min_hindfoot_length',
    'ave_hindfoot_length',
    'max_hindfoot_length',
    'min_weight',
    'ave_weight',
    'max_weight'
  ]

  return (
    <table>
      <tbody>
        <tr>{columns.map((c) => (<th>{c}</th>))}</tr>
        {data.filter(r => r).map((record) => {
          return (<tr>{columns.map((c) => (<td>{record[c]}</td>))}</tr>)
        })}
      </tbody>
    </table>
  )
}

export default DataDisplay
```

Like SurveyStats, DataDisplay returns a table listing the results returned from the server. Unlike SurveyStats, this component needs to check whether each record exists before it builds the table row. Remember that, when we defined how the year range query is handled in DataManager earlier, we told it to only return record objects for those years that have data. Here, we add `.filter(r => r)` before mapping the data to the callback to ensure that `DataDisplay` will only try to make `tr` elements from non-`null` records. We do the same when plotting the data.

15.6   THE CHART

We initially tried using Vega-Lite directly for the chart, but after a few failures and some online searching, we switched to `react-vega-lite`: Vega-Lite's `vega-embed` wants to modify an existing DOM element when called, while `react-vega-lite` constructs an element to be put in place at the right time, which proved easier to use. The steps are:

1. Create a paragraph placeholder if there's no data.
2. Re-organize non-`null` data into the form the chart needs.
3. Construct a spec like the ones we have seen before.
4. Create options to turn off the annoying links (also seen before).
5. Return an instance of the `VegaLite` component.

```
import React from 'react'
import VegaLite from 'react-vega-lite'

const DataChart = ({data}) => {
  if (! data) {
    return (<p>no data</p>)
  }

  const values = data
        .filter(r => r)
        .map(r => ({x: r.ave_hindfoot_length, y: r.ave_weight}))
  let spec = {
    '$schema': 'https://vega.github.io/schema/vega-lite/v2.0.json',
    'description': 'Mean Weight vs Mean Hindfoot Length',
    'mark': 'point',
    'encoding': {
      'x': {'field': 'x', 'type': 'quantitative'},
      'y': {'field': 'y', 'type': 'quantitative'}
    }
  }
  let options = {
    'actions': {
      'export': false,
      'source': false,
      'editor': false
    }
  }
  let scatterData = {
    'values': values
  }
  return (<VegaLite spec={spec} data={scatterData} options={options}/>)
}

export default DataChart
```

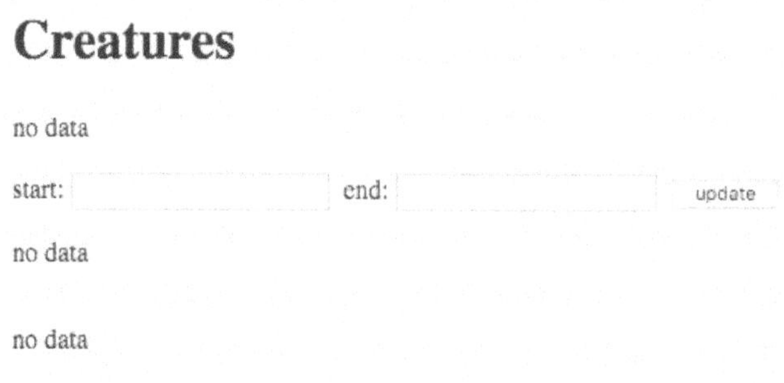

Creatures

no data

start: [   ]   end: [   ]   update

no data

no data

Figure 15.1: First Attempt at Viewing Capstone Project

The other components are similar to those we have seen before.

15.7 RUNNING IT

In order to test our application, we need to run a data server, and then launch our application with Parcel. The easiest way to do that is to open two windows on our computer and make each half the width (or height) of our screen so that we can see messages from both halves of what we're doing.

In one window, we run:

```
$ node src/capstone/back/driver-0.js src/capstone/back/test-data.csv
```

Note that we *don't* use npm run dev to trigger Parcel: this is running on the server, so no bundling is necessary.

In our other window, we run:

```
$ npm run dev src/capstone/front/index.html
```

which displays:

```
> js4ds@0.1.0 dev /Users/stj/js4ds
> parcel serve -p 4000 "src/capstone/front/index.html"

Server running at http://localhost:4000
+ Built in 20.15s.
```

We then open http://localhost:4000 in our browser and see Figure 15.1. That's unexpected: we should see the initial data displayed. If we open the console in the browser and reload the page, we see this error message:

```
Cross-Origin Request Blocked:
The Same Origin Policy disallows reading the remote resource \
  at http://localhost:3418/survey/stats.
(Reason: CORS header 'Access-Control-Allow-Origin' missing).
```

The "Learn More" link given with the error message takes us to this page[2], which uses many science words we don't know. A web search turns up this article on Wikipedia[3], which tells us that **cross-origin resource sharing** (CORS) is a security mechanism. If a page loads some JavaScript, and that JavaScript is allowed to send requests to servers other than the one that the page came from, then villains would be able to do things like send passwords saved in the browser to themselves. The details are too complex for this tutorial; the good news is that they've been wrapped up in a Node library called cors, which we can add to our server with just a couple of lines of code:

```
const express = require('express')
const cors = require('cors')          // added

let dataManager = null

const app = express()
app.use(cors())                       // added

app.get('/survey/stats', (req, res, next) => {
  // ...as before...
})

app.get('/survey/:start/:end', (req, res, next) => {
  // ...as before...
})

app.use((req, res, next) => {
  // ...as before...
})

module.exports = (dbm) => {
  // ...as before...
}
```

Since this code is saved in `server-1.js`, we need to create a copy of the driver called `driver-1.js` that invokes it. Let's run that:

```
$ node src/capstone/back/driver-1.js src/capstone/back/test-data.csv
```

and then re-launch our application to get Figure 15.2.

This is much better. We can now type some dates into the "start" and "end" boxes and, after we press "update", we get a chart and table of the aggregated statistics for the year range given (Figure 15.3).

We've built an interface, used it to submit queries that are then handled by a server, which returns data that can be converted to content by our React components, and our capstone project is complete.

---

[2]https://developer.mozilla.org/en-US/docs/Web/HTTP/CORS/Errors/CORSMissingAllowOrigin

[3]https://en.wikipedia.org/wiki/Cross-origin_resource_sharing

Creatures

record count 10
year low   1979
year high 2000

start: end: update

no data

no data

Figure 15.2: Second Attempt at Viewing Capstone Project

Creatures

record count 10
  year low   1979
  year high   2000

start: 1980-01-01   end: 1999-12-31   update

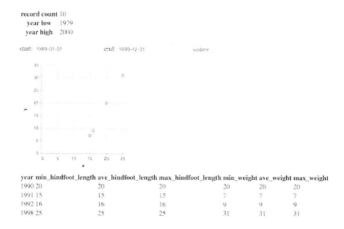

year	min_hindfoot_length	ave_hindfoot_length	max_hindfoot_length	min_weight	ave_weight	max_weight
1990 20	20	20	20	20	20	
1991 15	15	15	7	7	7	
1992 16	16	16	9	9	9	
1998 25	25	25	31	31	31	

Figure 15.3: Completed Capstone Project

15.8 EXERCISES

REPORTING OTHER DATA

A user has asked for the number of male and female animals observed for each year.

1. Should you add this to the existing query for yearly data or create a new API call?
2. Implement your choice.

ERROR CHECKING

1. Modify the server to return 400 with an error message if the range of years requested is invalid
2. Compare your implementation to someone else's. Did you define "invalid" in the same way, i.e., will your programs always return the same status codes for every query?

ADDING MORE TESTS

1. Our updated `server-1.js` doesn't have a test associated with it. Make a copy of `test-server.js` and adjust it to test this version of the server.
2. What other elements of the application could and should be tested? Try writing tests for those. In doing this, did you discover imperfections in the example code? If so, we'd love to hear about them (see Appendix C).

USE ALL THE DATA

Create a database using all of the survey data and test the display. What bugs or shortcomings do you notice compared to displaying test data?

MERGING DISPLAYS

The `SurveyStats` and `DataDisplay` components in the front end both display tables.

1. Write a new component `TableDisplay` that will display an arbitrary table given a list of column names and a list of objects which all have (at least) those fields.
2. Replace `SurveyStats` and `DataDisplay` with your new component.
3. Modify your component so that it generates a unique ID for each value in the table. (Hint: you may need to pass in a third parameter to each call to serve as the root or stem of those unique IDs.)

FORMATTING

Modify `DataDisplay` to format fractional numbers with a single decimal place, but leave the integers as they are. Ask yourself why, seven decades after the invention of digital computers, this isn't easier.

DATA, DATA EVERYWHERE

Modify `DataChart` so that the word `data` isn't used in so many different ways. Does doing this make you feel better about yourself as a person? Modify it again so that the height and width of the chart are passed in as well. Did that help?

KEY POINTS

- Use slices of actual data to test applications.
- Test summaries and small cases so that results can be checked by hand.
- Store state in a class, use pure functions to display it.

16 Finale

We have come a long way since `console.log('hello, world')` in Chapter 2. Callbacks and promises, JSON and web servers, packaging, unit tests, and visualization: every modern language can do them, but JavaScript is an increasingly popular choice. Yes, it has its flaws, but if we avoid some of the legacy features in Appendix G it's both usable and powerful.

Our journey doesn't stop here, though. The appendices explore some next steps, such as logging what our server does (Appendix I) and using a relational database (Appendix K) instead of a text file as a data store. Beyond that, you could look at more advanced techniques in JavaScript [Have2018], explore the full power of the D3[1] library for interactive visualization [Meek2017], dive into data wrangling [Davi2018], or start over completely the way JavaScript programmers do every eight months and rewrite everything with Web Components[2]. Whatever you do, we hope that this tutorial has helped you get started.

Contributions of all kinds are welcome, from errata and minor improvements to entirely new sections and chapters. Please file an issue[3] or submit a pull request[4] in our GitHub repository[5]. Everyone whose work is incorporated will be acknowledged. Please see the contributors' guide for more information, and please note that all contributors are required to abide by our Code of Conduct.

KEY POINTS

- We have learned a lot.
- Contributions are very welcome.

---

[1] https://d3js.org/

[2] https://developer.mozilla.org/en-US/docs/Web/Web_Components

[3] https://github.com/software-tools-in-javascript/js4ds/issues

[4] https://github.com/software-tools-in-javascript/js4ds/pulls

[5] https://github.com/software-tools-in-javascript/js4ds/

Bibliography

[Auro2018] Valerie Aurora and Mary Gardiner. *How to Respond to Code of Conduct Reports*. A practical step-by-step guide to handling code of conduct issues. Frame Shift Consulting, 2018.

[Davi2018] Ashley Davis. *Data Wrangling with JavaScript*. A step-by-step guide to managing data with JavaScript. Manning, 2018. ISBN: 978-1617294846.

[Foge2005] Karl Fogel. *Producing Open Source Software: How to Run a Successful Free Software Project*. The definitive guide to managing open source software development projects. O'Reilly Media, 2005. ISBN: 0596007590.

[Free1972] Jo Freeman. "The Tyranny of Structurelessness". In: *The Second Wave* 2.1 (1972). Points out that every organization has a power structure: the only question is whether it's accountable or not.

[Have2018] Martijn Haverbeke. *Eloquent Javascript*. 3rd. A widely-used programmer-oriented guide to modern JavaScript. No Starch Press, 2018. ISBN: 978-1593279509.

[Lind2008] Van Lindberg. *Intellectual Property and Open Source: A Practical Guide to Protecting Code*. A thorough dive into intellectual property issues related to open source software. O'Reilly Media, 2008. ISBN: 978-0596517960.

[Meek2017] Elijah Meeks. *D3.js in Action*. 2nd. A comprehensive guide to the D3 visualization framework. Manning, 2017. ISBN: 978-1617294488.

[Mina1986] Anne Minahan. "Martha's Rules". In: *Affilia* 1.2 (June 1986), pp. 53–56. DOI: 10.1177/088610998600100206.

[Mori2012] Andrew Morin, Jennifer Urban, and Piotr Sliz. "A Quick Guide to Software Licensing for the Scientist-Programmer". In: *PLoS Computational Biology* 8.7 (July 2012). A short introduction to software licensing for non-specialists. DOI: 10.1371/journal.pcbi.1002598.

[Wick2014] Hadley Wickham. "Tidy Data". In: *Journal of Statistical Software* 59.10 (2014). The defining paper on tidy data. DOI: 10.18637/jss.v059.i10.

[Wils2019] Greg Wilson. *Teaching Tech Together*. How to create and deliver lessons that work and build a teaching community around them. Taylor & Francis, 2019. ISBN: 978-0-367-35328-5.

A License

B Code of Conduct

In the interest of fostering an open and welcoming environment, we as contributors and maintainers pledge to making participation in our project and our community a harassment-free experience for everyone, regardless of age, body size, disability, ethnicity, gender identity and expression, level of experience, education, socio-economic status, nationality, personal appearance, race, religion, or sexual identity and orientation.

B.1 OUR STANDARDS

Examples of behavior that contributes to creating a positive environment include:

* using welcoming and inclusive language,
* being respectful of differing viewpoints and experiences,
* gracefully accepting constructive criticism,
* focusing on what is best for the community, and
* showing empathy towards other community members.

Examples of unacceptable behavior by participants include:

* the use of sexualized language or imagery and unwelcome sexual attention or advances,
* trolling, insulting/derogatory comments, and personal or political attacks,
* public or private harassment,
* publishing others' private information, such as a physical or electronic address, without explicit permission, and
* other conduct which could reasonably be considered inappropriate in a professional setting

B.2 OUR RESPONSIBILITIES

Project maintainers are responsible for clarifying the standards of acceptable behavior and are expected to take appropriate and fair corrective action in response to any instances of unacceptable behavior.

Project maintainers have the right and responsibility to remove, edit, or reject comments, commits, code, wiki edits, issues, and other contributions that are not aligned to this Code of Conduct, or to ban temporarily or permanently any contributor for other behaviors that they deem inappropriate, threatening, offensive, or harmful.

B.3 SCOPE

This Code of Conduct applies both within project spaces and in public spaces when
an individual is representing the project or its community. Examples of representing
a project or community include using an official project e-mail address, posting via
an official social media account, or acting as an appointed representative at an online
or offline event. Representation of a project may be further defined and clarified by
project maintainers.

B.4 ENFORCEMENT

Instances of abusive, harassing, or otherwise unacceptable behavior may be reported
by emailing the project team[1]. All complaints will be reviewed and investigated and
will result in a response that is deemed necessary and appropriate to the circumstances. The project team is obligated to maintain confidentiality with regard to the
reporter of an incident. Further details of specific enforcement policies may be posted
separately.

Project maintainers who do not follow or enforce the Code of Conduct in good
faith may face temporary or permanent repercussions as determined by other members of the project's leadership.

B.5 ATTRIBUTION

This Code of Conduct is adapted from the Contributor Covenant[2] version 1.4.

---

[1] gvwilson@third-bit.com

[2] https://www.contributor-covenant.org

C Contributing

Contributions of all kinds are welcome, from errata and minor improvements to entirely new sections and chapters: please submit an issue or pull request to our GitHub repository[1]. Everyone whose work is incorporated will be acknowledged; please note that all contributors are required to abide by our Code of Conduct (Appendix B). Please note that we use Simplified English rather than Traditional English, i.e., American rather than British spelling and grammar. We encourage translations; if you would like to take this on, please email us[2].

If you wish to report errata or suggest improvements to wording, please include the chapter name in the first line of the body of your report (e.g., `Testing Data Analysis`).

---

[1] https://github.com/software-tools-in-javascript/js4ds/

[2] gvwilson@third-bit.com

D Glossary

absolute path: A path that points to the same location in the filesystem regardless of where it's evaluated. An absolute path is the equivalent of latitude and longitude in geography. See also **relative path**.

aggregation function: A function that combines many values into one, such as sum or max.

alias: A second or subsequent name referring to the same data or function.

anonymous function: A function that is defined without giving it a name, such as a callback defined where it is used. Anonymous functions are sometimes called *lambda functions* because the Greek letter lambda is used for them in mathematics.

Application Programming Interface (API): the set of functions that a library or web service makes available for other code to use.

argument: see **parameter**.

array: A collection of values stored in a particular order and indexed numerically. Arrays are written as comma-separated values in square brackets, such as ['a', 'b', 'c']. The term **list** is often used synonymously.

ASCII: A widely-used set of numeric codes for representing characters from the Latin alphabet and common punctuation symbols, now superseded by **Unicode**.

assertion: A statement that something is true at a certain point in a program. Assertions are often used to define tests, but are also used in **production code** to check that software is behaving as it should.

attribute: A named property attached to an HTML **element**.

backward-compatible: Able to work consistently with older systems.

body (of an HTTP message): any optional data sent after the message's headers.

body (of a statement): The statements in a program that are nested within or controlled by another statement, such as those making up a function or those that are only executed if the **condition** of an if is true.

Boolean: A value that can be either true or false, named after the English mathematician George Boole (deceased).

bundler: A tool that combines JavaScript files, web pages, images, and other assets into a single bundle for deployment.

cache: A place where copies of recently-used values are stored for quicker access.

call stack: A data structure that stores information about function calls that are currently in progress. Each function call adds another table of variable-value pairs to the top of the stack; when the function completes, that table is discarded. See also **closure**.

callback function: A function A that is passed to another function B for B to call at a later time. Callback functions are used to implement delayed actions, such as what to do when data arrives in response to a network request.

Cascading Style Sheets (CSS): A way to describe how HTML should be rendered.

catch: To take responsibility for handling an **exception**. Catch is the counterpart of **throw**.

Creative Commons–Attribution License (CC-BY): A license that allows people to re-use work as long as they cite its original source.

character encoding: A specification of how characters are stored as bytes. The most commonly-used encoding today is **UTF-8**.

child class: A new **class** that **extends** an existing class (called the **parent class**).

child node: A **node** in a **tree** that is below some other node (which is called the child node's **parent**).

class: A programming structure that defines the properties and behavior of a family of related **objects**. Classes can **inherit** from other classes to specify or change behavior incrementally.

client: A program such as a browser that sends requests to a **server** and does something with the response. It is sometimes helpful to think of clients as sorcerers petitioning ancient gods for favors. Sometimes.

client-side page generation: To create an HTML page within a **client** using data provided by a **server**. See also **server-side page generation**.

closure: A set of variables defined in the same **scope** whose existence has been preserved after that scope has ended. Closures are one of the trickiest ideas in programming.

component (in React): A user-defined "tag" associated with a call to a function that generates HTML.

condition: The logical test that controls whether or not the **body** of an if statement executes or not.

constructor: A "method" that is automatically called to initialize an object when it is created.

Comma-Separated Values (CSV): A text format for tabular data in which each record is one row and fields are separated by commas. There are many minor variations, particularly around quoting of strings.

connection manager: An object that maintains a connection to a database. When the code is finished working with the database, the connection manager ensures that the connection is closed gracefully, which helps to avoid the corruption of data.

Content Delivery Network (CDN): A geographically distributed set of servers that store commonly-used or recently-used data such as web pages so that they can be served more quickly.

constant: a variable whose value cannot be changed. Note that the value itself might be changed: for example, after the statement const v = ['a', 'b'], the name v will always refer to the same array, but the array's contents can be changed. See also **variable**.

Cross-Origin Resource Sharing (CORS): A way to control requests made for data and other resources that aren't served by the site that gave the browser the original page.

dataframe: A data structure designed to store tabular data. A dataframe has zero or more named columns and zero or more rows, each of which has exactly one value for each column.

declarative programming: A style of programming in which the user specifies what they want, and the computer figures out how to deliver it.

deployment: The act of making software available for others to use.

destructuring: a form of assignment that unpacks a data structure in one step, such as [a, b] = [1, 2] or {left, right} = {left: 1, right: 2}.

Domain Name System (DNS): A decentralized naming system for computers that translates logical names such as third-bit.com into the addresses of particular computers.

document: An entire HTML page.

Document Object Model (DOM): A standard way to represent HTML in memory. The **elements** and **attributes** of the page, along with its text, are stored as **nodes** organized in a tree.

dotted notation: A common way to refer to the parts of structures in programming languages. whole.part means "the thing called part belonging to whole".

driver: A program that provides a standard interface through which to communicate with another piece of hardware or software. Every graphics card has a driver that translates generic drawing commands into card-specific operations; every database comes with drivers that (theoretically) allow other programs to talk to them all in the same way.

element: An individual component of a web page. In HTML, elements are enclosed in matching <tag> and </tag> pairs, or written as <tag/> if they contain no content. Elements are represented as **nodes** in the **DOM**.

entry point: A function with a known name and **signature** that a framework requires every plugin or other dynamically-loaded content to have. The entry point is (as the name suggests) how the framework gets into the plugin.

escape sequence: A sequence of characters used to represent some other character that would otherwise have a special meaning. For example, the escape sequence \" is used to represent a double-quote character inside a double-quoted string.

event handler: A **callback function** that does something in response to a particular interaction with a browser, such as a key being pressed or a link being clicked.

event listener: see **event handler**.

event loop: The fundamental processing cycle in JavaScript that takes the next task from a list and runs it, possibly adding more tasks to the list as it does so.

event object: An **object** that the system passes to an **event handler** that contains information about the event, such as which key was pressed.

exception: An object that stores information about an error or other unusual event in a program. One part of a program will create and **throw** an exception to signal that something unexpected has happened; another part will **catch** it.

extend: To create a new class from an existing class. We say that the new class **inherits** from the old one.

external style sheet: A set of **CSS** definitions placed in an external file rather than inside a web page. See also **internal style sheet**.

falsy: A horrible neologism meaning "equivalent to false". See also the equally horrible **truthy**.

fat arrow function: A function defined using `(parameters) => {body}`. Fat arrow functions treat the special value `this` in a less inconsistent way than their older equivalents.

field: A named part of a **record** in a **relational database**. Fields are typically shown as columns in a **table**.

fixture: The data on which a **unit test** is run.

functional programming: A style of programming in which data is transformed through successive application of functions, rather than by using control structures such as loops. Functional programming in JavaScript relies heavily on **callbacks** and **higher-order functions**.

global installation: A JavaScript library placed in a location where it can be accessed by all users and projects. See also **local installation**.

global variable: A variable defined outside any particular function, which is therefore visible to all functions. See also **local variable**.

GNU Public License (GPL): A license that allows people to re-use software as long as they distribute the source of their changes.

header row: If present, the first of a **CSV** file that defines column names (but tragically, not their data types or units).

heterogeneous: Having mixed type. For example, an **array** is said to be heterogeneous if it contains a mix of numbers, character strings, and values of other types. See also **homogeneous**.

higher-order function: A function that operates on other functions. For example, the higher-order function `forEach` executes a given function once on each value in an **array**. Higher-order functions are heavily used in **functional programming**.

homogeneous: Having a single type. For example, an **array** is said to be homogeneous if it contains only numbers or only character strings, but not a mix of the two.

hostname: The part of a URL that specifies the computer to talk to. In the URL `http://example.com/something/`, the hostname is `example.com`; in the URL `http://localhost:1234/`, it is `localhost`.

HyperText Transfer Protocol (HTTP): The HyperText Transfer Protocol used to exchange information between browsers and websites, and more generally between other **clients** and **servers**. HTTP is a **stateless** protocol in which communication consists of **requests** and **responses**.

HTTP header: A name-value pair at the start of an HTTP **request** or **response**. Headers are used to specify what data formats the sender can handle, the date and time the message was sent, and so on.

HTTP method: The verb in an **HTTP request** that defines what the client wants to do. Common methods are GET (to get data) and POST (to submit data).

HTTP request: A precisely-formatted block of text sent from a **client** (such as a browser) to a **server** that specifies what resource is being requested, what data formats the client will accept, and so on.

HTTP response: A precisely-formatted block of text sent from a **server** back to a **client** in reply to a **request**.

HTTP status code: A numerical code that indicates what happened when an **HTTP request** was processed, such as 200 (OK), 404 (not found), or 500 (internal server error).

immutable: Data that cannot be changed after being created.

in-memory database: A database that is stored in memory rather than in permanent storage. In-memory databases are often used for testing.

inherit: To acquire properties and methods from a parent class. See also **extend**.

inner loop: A loop contained in the **body** of another loop. See also **nested loop**.

instance: If an object `obj` is of a particular class `cls`, we say that `obj` is an instance of `cls`.

instance method: A method that is called using, and operates on, a particular object. See also **static method**.

internal style sheet: A set of **CSS** definitions placed inside a web page rather than in an external file. See also **external style sheet**.

JavaScript Object Notation (JSON): A way to represent data by combining basic values like numbers and character strings in **arrays** and name/value structures. The acronym stands for "JavaScript Object Notation"; unlike better-defined standards like **XML**, it is unencumbered by a syntax for comments or ways to define **schemas**.

library: see **module**.

list: see **array**.

local installation: A JavaScript library placed inside a particular project, and only accessible within that project. See also **global installation**.

local server: A **server** run on the user's own computer, usually for testing purposes during development.

local variable: A variable defined inside a function which is only visible within that function. See also **global variable** and **closure**.

logging: To record information about a program's execution in a structured way.

logging transport: A channel through which **logging** messages are sent, such as standard output (for the user's screen) or a database connection.

member variable: see **property**.

memory diagram: A picture showing the variables a program contains and the data they refer to.

method: A function attached to an **object**, typically called using **dotted notation**. In JavaScript and many other languages, a special variable called this is provided to methods to refer to the particular object for which the method is being called.

method chaining: A style of programming in which each method call returns either the original object or a newly-constructed object so that other method calls can be appended to create long chains of calculations. Method chaining produces code that looks like obj.a().b().c().

minimization: To remove spaces and other extraneous characters from source files (and possibly even rename variables). This makes those files smaller and faster to deploy at the expense of readability.

MIT License: A license that allows people to re-use software with no restrictions.

model (of data): How data is stored. See also **view**.

module: A set of variables, functions, and/or classes grouped together for easier management (typically but not always in a single file). Modules are sometimes also called **libraries**.

module variable: A variable that is visible within a module but not outside it. See also **scope**.

mutation: Changing data in place, such as modifying an element of an array or adding a record to a database.

name collision: The ambiguity that arises when two or more things in a program that have the same name are active at the same time. The **call stack** was invented in part to address this problem.

nested loop: A loop that is contained in another loop. The **inner loop** can run many times for each iteration of the **outer loop**.

Node: An open source implementation of JavaScript for use outside the browser.

node: An in-memory representation of an element in an HTML page (not to be confused with **Node.js**). See also **DOM**.

NoSQL database: Any database that doesn't use the **relational** model. The awkward name comes from the fact that such databases don't use **SQL** as a query language.

Not a Number (NaN): A special value used to represent an invalid number, such as the result of dividing zero by zero.

object: A clump of variables and/or **methods** grouped together in a program. In most languages, objects can only be created as instances of **classes,** but JavaScript calls anything created using {...} an object. Do not seek to walk in the footsteps of the sages; seek rather what they sought.

object-oriented programming (OOP): A style of programming centered around constructing self-contained objects that communicate through well-defined (or at least "defined") interfaces.

observer-observable: A widely-used programming pattern in which some **objects** are notified and take action when other objects change state or take action.

outer loop: A loop that contains another loop. See also **nested loop.**

override: to replace a definition of a **method** in a **parent-class** with a new definition in a **child class.**

query parameter: A placeholder in an **SQL** query that must be filled in with an actual value in order for the query to run.

package manager: A program that does its best to keep track of the bits and bobs of software installed on a computer. The most widely used package manager for JavaScript is called NPM; it does its best, but really, without proper discipline on the part of programmers, it's like Boromir trying to hold back the orcs or a kindergarten teacher trying to keep everyone's shirt clean during finger-painting.

parameter: A variable whose value is passed into a function when the function is called. Some writers distinguish parameters (the variables) from **arguments** (the values passed in), but others use the terms in the opposite sense. It's all very confusing.

parent class: An existing **class** that has been **extended** to create a new class. (The new class is called the **child class.**)

parent node: The **node** in a **tree** that is above some other node. Every node has a parent except the **root node.**

parsing: To translate the text of a program or web page into a data structure in memory that the program can then manipulate.

polymorphism: Literally, "having many forms". The term refers to the way in which **objects** whose **methods** have the same names and **parameters** can be used interchangeably.

port: A logical endpoint for communication, like a phone number in an office building. In the URL `http://example.com:8081/something`, the port is `8081`. Only one program may use a port at any time.

production code: Software that is delivered to an end user. The term is used to distinguish such code from test code, deployment infrastructure, and everything else that programmers write along the way.

promise: A way to handle delayed computations in JavaScript. Promises were supposed to make programmers' lives simpler.

prototype: An idiosyncratic mechanism used in the original definition of JavaScript for sharing properties between objects that we unfortunately still have to cope with.

property: A variable associated with an **object**. The term is used to distinguish an object's passive data from its executable **methods**. Properties are sometimes called **member variables**.

pseudo-random number: A value generated in a repeatable way that has the properties of being truly random.

pseudo-random number generator: A function that can generate a series of **pseudo-random numbers** after being initialized with a **seed**.

public domain license (CC-0): A license that allows people to re-use material however they want with no restrictions and no requirement of attribution.

race condition: A situation in which the result of a computation can vary due to operations being performed in different orders.

raise: see **throw**.

refactor: To reorganize or clean up code in a way that doesn't change its behavior.

read-evaluate-print loop (REPL): An interactive program that reads a command typed in by a user, executes it, prints the result, and then waits patiently for the next command. REPLs are often used to explore new ideas or for debugging.

record: A set of related values. In a **relational database**, a record is typically shown as a single row in a **table**. See also **field**.

regular expression: A pattern for matching text, written as text itself. Regular expressions are sometimes called "regexp", "regex", or "RE", and are as powerful as they are cryptic.

relational database: A database that organizes information into **tables**, each of which has a fixed set of named **fields** (shown as columns) and a variable number of **records** (shown as rows). See also **SQL**.

relative path: A path whose destination is interpreted relative to some other location, such as the current directory. A relative path is the equivalent of giving directions using terms like "straight" and "left". See also **absolute path**.

responsive design: An approach to building web pages and other applications that resizes and reorganizes things smoothly for different sizes of screens.

RGB: A way to represent colors as triples of red, green, and blue intensities, each of which ranges from 0 to 255. RGB is often augmented in modern systems to create RGBA, where the fourth component is the pixel's transparency.

root: The only node in a **tree** that *doesn't* have a **parent**.

root directory: The directory that contains everything else, directly or indirectly. The root directory is written / (a bare forward slash).

root element: The **element** in a document that contains every other element. The root element of a web page is the html element.

schema: A specification of the "shape" of data, such as the **fields** making up a database table or the ways in which structures can be nested in **JSON**.

scope: The portion of a program within which a definition can be seen and used. See also **global-variable**, **local-variable**, **module-variable**, and (if you are brave) **closure**.

seed: A value used to initialize a **pseudo-random number generator**.

selector: A way to identify elements within an HTML document. The selector h2#contents, for example, means "the h2 element with the ID contents".

server: A program that waits for requests from **clients** and sends them data in response. It is sometimes helpful to think of servers as harassed parents trying to babysit a room full of unruly children.

server-side page generation: To create an HTML page on a server. That HTML is then delivered as-is to a browser for display. See also **client-side page generation**.

spread syntax: The ... in ...some_array, which means "interpolate the values of the array in place".

SQL: The language used for writing queries for **relational databases**. The term was originally an acronym for Structured Query Language.

signature: The ordered list of argument data types required by a function or **method**. If two functions or methods have the same signature, they can be called in the same way.

stateful: To retain information from one operation to the next.

stateless: To *not* retain information from one operation to the next.

static method: one that belongs to the class as a whole rather than to objects of that class. Static methods are often used to implement helper methods for classes. See also **instance method**.

string: A block of text in a program. The term is short for "character string".

string interpolation: The process of inserting text corresponding to specified values into a string, usually to make output human-readable.

table: A set of uniformly-formatted **records** in a **relational database**. Tables are usually drawn with rows (each of which represents one record) and columns (each of which represents a **field**).

tag: A short textual label identifying a kind of element in an HTML page. Commonly-used tags include p (for a paragraph) and h1 (for a level-1 heading).

template: A document with some placeholders that can be filled in with specific values. Templates are often used to create personalized email messages and web pages, though their efficacy is predicated upon relentless commercialization and devaluation of modern society's sense of what constitutes "personal".

test runner: A program that finds and runs **unit tests** and reports their results.

test suite: A set of **unit tests**, usually stored in files that follow a prescribed naming convention.

throw: To signal that something unexpected or unusual has happened in a program by creating an **exception** and handing it to the error-handling system, which then tries to find a point in the program that will **catch** it. (Some languages call this *raising* an exception.)

tidy data: Tabular data that satisfies four conditions:
- Each column contains one statistical variable (i.e., one property that was measured or observed).
- Each different observation is in a different row.
- There is one table for each set of observations.
- If there are multiple tables, each table has a column containing a unique key so that related data can be linked.

tree: A data structure containing strictly-nested **nodes**. Every node except the **root node** must have exactly one **parent node**, but each node may have zero or more **children**.

truthy: A truly Orwellian neologism meaning "not equivalent to false". See also **falsy**, but only if you are able to set aside your respect for the English language.

Unicode: A standard that defines numeric codes for many thousands of characters and symbols. Unicode does *not* define how those numbers are stored; that is done by standards like **UTF-8**.

unit test: A test that exercises one property or expected behavior of a system.

URL: A multi-part identifier that specifies something on a computer network. A URL may contain a protocol (such as `http`), a hostname (such as `example.com`), a port (such as `80`), a path (such as `/homepage.html`), and **query parameters**.

UTF-8: A way to store the numeric codes representing Unicode characters in memory that is **backward-compatible** with the older **ASCII** standard.

variable: A name in a program that has some data associated with it. A variable's value can be changed after definition. See also **constant**.

view (of data): How data is presented. See also **model**.

whitespace: The space, newline, carriage return, and horizontal and vertical tab characters that take up space but don't create a visible mark. The name comes from their appearance on a printed page in the era of typewriters.

XML: A set of rules for defining HTML-like tags and using them to format documents (typically data). XML achieved license plate popularity in the early 2000s, but its complexity led many programmers to adopt **JSON** instead.

E Key Points

INTRODUCTION

- Modern JavaScript is a good tool for building desktop and web-based applications.
- This course is for people who know what loops and functions are, but have never used JavaScript or built web applications.
- Node is a command-line interpreter for JavaScript, which can be used interactively or to run scripts in files.
- NPM is the Node Package Manager, which can be used to find, install, update, build, and execute JavaScript libraries.

BASIC FEATURES

- Use `console.log` to print messages.
- Use dotted notation `X.Y` to get part `Y` of object `X`.
- Basic data types are Booleans, numbers, and character strings.
- Arrays store multiple values in order.
- The special values `null` and `undefined` mean 'no value' and 'does not exist'.
- Define constants with `const` and variables with `let`.
- `typeof` returns the type of a value.
- `for (let variable of collection) {...}` iterates through the values in an array.
- `if (condition) {...} else {...}` conditionally executes some code.
- `false`, 0, the empty string, `null`, and `undefined` are false; everything else is true.
- Use back quotes and `${...}` to interpolate values into strings.
- An object is a collection of name/value pairs written in `{...}`.
- `object[key]` or `object.key` gets a value from an object.
- Functions are objects that can be assigned to variables, stored in lists, etc.
- `function name(...parameters...) {...body...}` is the old way to define a function.
- `name = (...parameters...) => {...body...}` is the new way to define a function.
- Use `return` inside a function body to return a value at any point.
- Use modules to divide code between multiple files for re-use.
- Assign to `module.exports` to specify what a module exports.
- `require(...path...)` imports a module.
- Paths beginning with '.' or '/' are imported locally, but paths without '.' or '/' look in the library.

CALLBACKS

- JavaScript stores the instructions making up a function in memory like any other object.
- Function objects can be assigned to variables, put in lists, passed as arguments to other functions, etc.
- Functions can be defined in place without ever being given a name.
- A callback function is one that is passed in to another function for it to execute at a particular moment.
- Functional programming uses higher-order functions on immutable data.
- `Array.some` is true if any element in an array passes a test, while `Array.every` is true if they all do.
- `Array.filter` selects elements of an array that pass a test.
- `Array.map` creates a new array by transforming values in an existing one.
- `Array.reduce` reduces an array to a single value.
- A closure is a set of variables captured during the definition of a function.

OBJECTS AND CLASSES

- Create classes to define combinations of data and behavior.
- Use the class's constructor to initialize objects.
- `this` refers to the current object.
- Use polymorphism to express common behavior patterns.
- Extend existing classes to create new ones-sometimes.
- Override methods to change or extend their behavior.

HTML AND CSS

- HTML is the latest in a long line of markup languages.
- HTML documents contain elements (represented by tags in angle brackets) and text.
- Elements must be strictly nested.
- Elements can contain attributes.
- Use escape sequences beginning with ampersand to represent special characters.
- Every page should have one `html` element containing a `head` and a `body`.
- Use `<!--...-->` to include comments in HTML.
- Use `ul` and `ol` for unordered and ordered lists, and `li` for list elements.
- Use `table` for tables, `tr` for rows, `th` for headings, and `td` for regular data.
- Use `<a href="...">...</a>` to create links.
- Use `<img src="..." title="..." alt="..." />` to include images.
- Use CSS to define appearance of elements.
- Use `class` and `id` to identify elements.
- Use selectors to specify the elements that CSS applies to.

MANIPULATING PAGES

- Use a `meta` tag in a page's header to specify the page's character encoding.
- Pages are represented in memory using a Document Object Model (DOM).
- The `document` object represents the page a script is in.
- Use the `querySelectorAll` method to find DOM nodes that match a condition.
- Assign HTML text to a node's `innerHTML` property to change the node's content.
- Use `((params) => {...})(arguments)` to create and call a function in a single step.
- An event listener is a function run by the browser when some specific event occurs.
- Create an event listener for `'DOMContentLoaded'` to trigger execution of scripts *after* the DOM has been constructed.
- Check the `nodeType` or `nodeName` property of a DOM node to find out what kind of node it is.
- Destructuring assignment allows us to assign to multiple variables by name in a single statement.
- Use `setTimeout` to trigger execution of a function after a delay.
- To make something run forever, have the function called by `setTimeout` set another timeout of the same function.

DYNAMIC PAGES

- Older dynamic web sites generated pages on the server.
- Newer dynamic web sites generate pages in the client.
- React is a JavaScript library for client-side page generation that represents HTML elements as function calls.
- React replaces page elements with dynamically-generated content in memory (not on disk).
- React functions can be customized with elements.
- JSX translates HTML into React function calls so that HTML and JavaScript can be mixed freely.
- Use Babel to translate JSX into JavaScript in the browser.
- Define new React components with a pseudo-HTML element and a corresponding function.
- Attributes to pseudo-HTML are passed to the JavaScript function as a `props` object.

VISUALIZING DATA

- Vega-Lite is a simple way to build common visualizations.
- Vega-Lite is declarative: the user creates a data structure describing what they want, and the library creates the visualization.
- A Vega-Lite specification contains a schema identifier, a description, data, marks, and encodings.

- The overall layout of a Vega-Lite visualization can be controlled by setting options.
- Some applications will use `require` for server-side code and `import` for client-side code.

PROMISES

- JavaScript keeps an execution queue for delayed computations.
- Use promises to manage delayed computation instead of raw callbacks.
- Use a callback with two arguments to handle successful completion (resolve) and unsuccessful completion (reject) of a promise.
- Use `then` to express the next step after successful completion and `catch` to handle errors.
- Use `Promise.all` to wait for all promises in a list to complete and `Promise.race` to wait for the first promise in a set to complete.
- Use `await` to wait for the result of a computation.
- Mark functions that can be waited on with `async`.

INTERACTIVE SITES

- Define event handlers to specify what actions the browser should take when the user interacts with an application.
- The browser passes event objects containing details of events to event handlers.
- Use classes to keep state and event handlers together.
- React calls a class's `render` to display it.
- Separate models (which store data) from views (which display it).
- Use `fetch` to get data from servers.
- Use destructuring to get individual members from an object in a single step.
- Modern JavaScript uses promises to manage asynchronous activities.

MANAGING DATA

- Small tabular datasets are commonly stored as Comma-Separated Values (CSV).
- CSV can only represent regular data, and CSV files usually don't include units.
- Nested data is commonly stored using JavaScript Object Notation (JSON).
- JSON representations of tabular data often include redundant (and therefore possibly inconsistent) specifications of column names.
- PapaParse is a robust CSV parsing library that produces JSON output.

CREATING A SERVER

- An HTTP request or response consists of a plain-text header and an optional body.
- HTTP is a stateless protocol.
- Express provides a simple path-based JavaScript server.
- Write callback functions to handle requests matching specified paths.

- Provide a default handler for unrecognized requests.
- Use `Content-Type` to specify the type of data being returned.
- Use dynamic loading to support plugin extensions.

TESTING

- A unit test checks the behavior of one software component in isolation.
- The result of a unit test can be pass, fail, or error.
- Use Mocha to write and run unit tests in JavaScript.
- Put assertions in unit tests to check results.
- Combine tests in suites for easier management.
- Divide modules into interactive and non-interactive parts for easier testing.
- Use `supertest` to simulate interaction with a server for testing.
- HTML is represented in memory using the Document Object Model (DOM).
- Check the structure of the DOM rather than the textual representation of the HTML when testing.

USING DATA-FORGE

- Create a `DataFrame` from an array of objects with identical keys, from a spec with `columnNames` and `rows` fields, or by parsing text that contains CSV or JSON.
- If you're using a loop on a dataframe, you're doing the wrong thing.
- Use method chaining to create pipelines that filter data and create new values from old.
- Use grouping and aggregation to summarize data.

CAPSTONE PROJECT

- Use slices of actual data to test applications.
- Test summaries and small cases so that results can be checked by hand.
- Store state in a class, use pure functions to display it.

FINALE

- We have learned a lot.
- Contributions are very welcome.

F Collaborating

A project can survive badly-organized code; none will survive for long if people are confused, pulling in different directions, or hostile. This appendix therefore talks about what projects can do to make newcomers feel welcome and to make things run smoothly after that.

It may seem strange to include this material in a tutorial on JavaScript, but as Freeman pointed out in **[Free1972]**, every group has a power structure; the only question is whether it is formal and accountable or informal and unaccountable. Thirty-five years after the free software movement took on its modern, self-aware form, its successes and failures have shown that if a project doesn't clearly state who has the right to do what, it will wind up being run by whoever argues loudest and longest. For a much deeper discussion of these issues, see **[Foge2005]**.

F.1 LICENSING SOFTWARE

If the law or a publication agreement prevents people from reading your work or using your software, you're probably hurting your own career. You may need to do this in order to respect personal or commercial confidentiality, but the first and most important rule of inclusivity is to be open by default.

That is easier said than done, not least because the law hasn't kept up with everyday practice. **[Mori2012]** and this blog post[1] are good starting points from a scientist's point of view, while **[Lind2008]** is a deeper dive for those who want details. In brief, creative works are automatically eligible for intellectual property (and thus copyright) protection. This means that every creative work has some sort of license: the only question is whether authors and users know what it is.

Every project should therefore include an explicit license. This license should be chosen early: if you don't set it up right at the start, then each collaborator will hold copyright on their work and will need to be asked for approval when a license *is* chosen. By convention, the license is usually put in a file called LICENSE or LICENSE.txt in the project's root directory. This file should clearly state the license(s) under which the content is being made available; the plural is used because code, data, and text may be covered by different licenses.

Don't Write Your Own License
Not even if you are a lawyer: legalese is a highly technical language, and words don't mean what you think they do.

To make license selection as easy as possible, GitHub allows you to select one of the most common licenses when creating a repository. The Open Source Initiative

---

[1] http://www.astrobetter.com/blog/2014/03/10/the-whys-and-hows-of-licensing-scientific-code/

maintains a list of licenses[2], and choosealicense.com[3] will help you find a license that suits your needs. Some of the things you will need to think about are:

1. Do you want to license the code at all?
2. Is the content you are licensing source code?
3. Do you require people distributing derivative works to also distribute their code?
4. Do you want to address patent rights?
5. Is your license compatible with the licenses of the software you depend on? For example, as we will discuss below, you can use MIT-licensed code in a GPL-licensed project but not vice versa.

The two most popular licenses for software are the **MIT license** and the **GNU Public License** (GPL). The MIT license (and its close sibling the BSD license) say that people can do whatever they want to with the software as long as they cite the original source, and that the authors accept no responsibility if things go wrong. The GPL gives people similar rights, but requires them to share their own work on the same terms:

You may copy, distribute and modify the software as long as you track changes/dates in source files. Any modifications to or software including (via compiler) GPL-licensed code must also be made available under the GPL along with build & install instructions.
— tl;dr[4]

We recommend the MIT license: it places the fewest restrictions on future action, it can be made stricter later on, and the last thirty years show that it's good enough to keep work open.

F.2 LICENSING DATA AND DOCUMENTATION

The MIT license and the GPL apply to software. When it comes to data and reports, the most widely used family of licenses are those produced by Creative Commons[5], which have been written and checked by lawyers and are well understood by the community.

The most liberal license is referred to as **CC-0**, where the "0" stands for "zero restrictions". CC-0 puts work in the public domain, i.e., allows anyone who wants to use it to do so however they want with no restrictions. This is usually the best choice for data, since it simplifies aggregate analysis. For example, if you choose a license for data that requires people to cite their source, then anyone who uses that data in

---

[2]http://opensource.org/licenses

[3]http://choosealicense.com/

[4]https://tldrlegal.com/license/gnu-general-public-license-v3-(gpl-3)

[5]https://creativecommons.org/

an analysis must cite you; so must anyone who cites *their* results, and so on, which quickly becomes unwieldy.

The next most common license is the Creative Commons–Attribution license, usually referred to as **CC-BY**. This allows people to do whatever they want to with the work as long as they cite the original source. This is the best license to use for manuscripts, since you *want* people to share them widely but also want to get credit for your work.

Other Creative Commons licenses incorporate various restrictions on specific use cases:

- ND (no derivative works) prevents people from creating modified versions of your work. Unfortunately, this also inhibits translation and reformatting.
- NC (no commercial use) does *not* mean that people cannot charge money for something that includes your work, though some publishers still try to imply that in order to scare people away from open licensing. Instead, the NC clause means that people cannot charge for something that uses your work without your explicit permission, which you can give under whatever terms you want.
- Finally, SA (share-alike) requires people to share work that incorporates yours on the same terms that you used. Again, this is fine in principle, but in practice makes aggregation a headache.

F.3   CODE OF CONDUCT

You don't expect to have a fire, but every large building or event should have a fire safety plan. Similarly, having a Code of Conduct like Appendix B for your project reduces the uncertainty that participants face about what is acceptable and unacceptable behavior. You might think this is obvious, but long experience shows that articulating it clearly and concisely reduces problems caused by having different expectations, particularly when people from very different cultural backgrounds are trying to collaborate. An explicit Code of Conduct is particularly helpful for newcomers, so having one can help your project grow and encourage people to give you feedback.

Having a Code of Conduct is particularly important for people from marginalized or under-represented groups, who have probably experienced harassment or unwelcoming behavior before. By adopting one, you signal that your project is trying to be a better place than YouTube, Twitter, and other online cesspools. Some people may push back claiming that it's unnecessary, or that it infringes freedom of speech, but in our experience, what they often mean is that thinking about how they might have benefited from past inequity makes them feel uncomfortable, or that they like to argue for the sake of arguing. If having a Code of Conduct leads to them going elsewhere, that will probably make your project run more smoothly.

Just as you shouldn't write your own license for a project, you probably shouldn't write your own Code of Conduct. We recommend using the Contributor Covenant[6]

---

[6]https://www.contributor-covenant.org

for development projects and the model code of conduct[7] from the Geek Feminism Wiki[8] for in-person events. Both have been thought through carefully and revised in the light of experience, and both are now used widely enough that many potential participants in your project will not need to have them explained.

Rules are meaningless if they aren't enforced. If you adopt a Code of Conduct, it is therefore important to be clear about how to report issues and who will handle them. **[Auro2018]** is a short, practical guide to handling incidents; like the Contributor Covenant and the model code of conduct, it's better to start with something that other people have thought through and refined than to try to create something from scratch.

F.4 GOVERNANCE

If your project involves more than half a dozen people, you should be explicit about the way decisions are made. We recommend Martha's Rules **[Mina1986]**:

1. Before each meeting, anyone who wishes may sponsor a proposal. Proposals must be circulated at least 24 hours before a meeting in order to be considered at that meeting, and must include:

   * a one-line summary (the subject line of the issue);
   * the full text of the proposal;
   * any required background information;
   * pros and cons; and
   * possible alternatives.

2. A quorum is established in a meeting if half or more of voting members are present.
3. Once a person has sponsored a proposal, they are responsible for it. The group may not discuss or vote on the issue unless the sponsor or their delegate is present. The sponsor is also responsible for presenting the item to the group.
4. After the sponsor presents the proposal, a *sense vote* is cast for the proposal prior to any discussion:

   * Who likes the proposal?
   * Who can live with the proposal?
   * Who is uncomfortable with the proposal?

5. If all or most of the group likes or can live with the proposal, it is immediately moved to a formal vote with no further discussion.
6. If most of the group is uncomfortable with the proposal, it is postponed for further rework by the sponsor.

---

[7]http://geekfeminism.wikia.com/wiki/Conference_anti-harassment/Policy

[8]http://geekfeminism.wikia.com/

7. If some members are uncomfortable they can briefly state their objections. A timer is then set for a brief discussion moderated by the facilitator. After 10 minutes or when no one has anything further to add (whichever comes first), the facilitator calls for a yes-or-no vote on the question: "Should we implement this decision over the stated objections?" If a majority votes "yes" the proposal is implemented. Otherwise, the proposal is returned to the sponsor for further work.

G Legacy JavaScript Issues

JavaScript is now twenty-five years old, and like many twenty-somethings, it is still struggling with issues from its childhood. This appendix explores three of them.

G.1 EQUALITY

Gary Bernhardt's lightning talk from 2012[1] may be the most-watched presentation on JavaScript ever. In it, he rattles through some truths about the language that may surprise you (Table G.1).

Operation	Code	Result
empty array plus empty array	`[] + []`	`""` (empty string)
empty array plus empty object	`[] + {}`	`{}` (empty object)
empty object plus empty array	`{} + []`	`0` (number zero)
empty object plus empty object	`{} + {}`	`NaN` (not a number)

Table G.1: Surprising Results

In order to understand this, we need to know several things (which are laid out in more detail in this article[2] by Abhinav Suri):

1. Arrays are objects whose keys happen to be sequential integers.
2. When JavaScript tries to add things that aren't numbers, it tries to convert them to numbers, and if that doesn't work, to strings (because it can always concatenate strings).
3. To convert an array to a string, JavaScript converts the elements to strings and concatenates them. If the array is empty, the result is an empty string.
4. When converting an object to a string, JavaScript produces `[object CLASS]`, where CLASS is the name of the object's class.
5. `{}` can be interpreted as either an empty object *or* an empty block of code.

So:

- Empty array plus empty array becomes empty string plus empty string.
- Empty array plus empty object becomes empty string plus `[object Object]` (because the class of an empty object is just `Object`).

---

[1] https://www.destroyallsoftware.com/talks/wat

[2] https://medium.com/dailyjs/the-why-behind-the-wat-an-explanation-of-javascripts-weird-type-system-83b92879a8db

- `{} + []` is "an empty block of code producing nothing, followed by `+[]`", which becomes "+ of the numeric value of the string value of an empty array", which becomes "+ of 0".
- Empty object plus empty object is interpreted as an empty object plus an empty block of code, and since an empty block of code doesn't produce a result, its "value" is `NaN` (not a number).

This is one of many cases in programming (and real life) where doing something that's convenient in a simple case produces confusion in less common cases. Every language except Canadian English has warts like these.

G.2 ITERATION

We wrote above that arrays are objects. This led to some undesirable behavior with JavaScript's original `for` loop, which used the word `in` rather than `of`, and which looped over all of an object's enumerable keys:

```
const things = ['x', 'y', 'z']
things.someProperty = 'someValue'

for (let key in things) {
  console.log(key)
}
```

```
0
1
2
someProperty
```

That phrase "enumerable keys" conceals some strangeness of its own, but in brief, a `for-in` loop will loop over keys inherited from the object's parents as well as those defined in the object itself. Since this is usually not what programmers want (especially for arrays), older code often used a C-style loop:

```
for (let i = 0; i < things.length; i += 1) {
  console.log(i)
}
```

```
0
1
2
```

Today's solution is to use `for-of` to get the *values* from an array, which is usually what we want:

```
for (let key of things) {
  console.log(key)
}
```

```
x
y
z
```

Better yet, use `forEach` and take advantage of its optional second and third arguments:

```
things.forEach((val, loc, array) => {
    console.log(`element ${loc} of ${array} is ${val}`)
})
```

```
element 0 of x,y,z is x
element 1 of x,y,z is y
element 2 of x,y,z is z
```

G.3 PROTOTYPES

We come finally to an aspect of JavaScript that has been the cause of a great deal of confusion: prototypes. Every JavaScript object has an internal property called its **prototype**. If you try to access some property of an object and it's not found, JavaScript automatically looks in the object that the first object's prototype refers to. If the desired property isn't there, JavaScript looks in the prototype object's prototype, and so on.

So where do prototypes come from? If an object is created with `new Something()`, and the function `Something` has a property called `prototype`, then the new object's prototype is set to the object to which that `prototype` property points.

This will all make sense with an example and a diagram. Let's create an object to store the default properties of ice cream cones, then create a function `Cone` that creates an actual cone:

```
const iceCream = {
    size: 'large'
}

const Cone = function(f) {
    this.flavor = f
}

Cone.prototype = iceCream
```

We can now create a cone and look at its properties (Figure G.1):

```
const dessert = new Cone('mustard')
console.log(`flavor "${dessert.flavor}" size "${dessert.size}"`)
```

```
flavor "mustard" size "large"
```

If we change the `size` of our dessert, lookup finds the object's property before looking up the chain to find the parent object's:

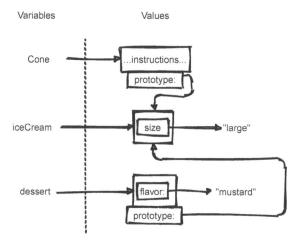

Figure G.1: Prototypes

```
dessert.size = 'extra-large'
console.log(`new flavor "${dessert.flavor}" size "${dessert.size}"`)
```

```
new flavor "mustard" size "extra-large"
```

Prototypes are a way to implement inheritance for object-oriented programming; the problem is that the mechanics are rather clumsy, and very different from what most programmers are used to, so people built a variety of layers on top of prototypes. To make things even more confusing, this can behave in some rather odd ways, and again, people built layers to try to insulate themselves from those oddities. Prototypes still have their fans, but most people find modern JavaScript's classes easier to use.

H Regular Expressions

A **regular expression** is a pattern for matching text. Most languages implement them in libraries, but they are built into JavaScript, and are written using / before and after a string rather than single or double quotes.

- Letters and digits match themselves, so the regular expression /enjoy/ matches the word "enjoy" wherever it appears in a string.
- A dot matches any character, so /../ matches any two consecutive characters and /en..y/ matches "enjoy", "gently", and "brightens your day".
- The asterisk * means "match zero or more occurrences of what comes immediately before", so en* matches "ten" and "penny". It also matches "feet" (which has an "e" followed by zero occurrences of "n").
- The plus sign + means "match *one* or more occurrences of what comes immediately before", so en+ still matches "ten" and "penny" but doesn't match "feet" (because there isn't an "n").
- Parentheses create groups just as they do in mathematics, so (an)+ matches "banana" but not "annual".
- The pipe character | means "either/or", so b|c matches either a single "b" or a single "c", and (either)|(or) matches either "either" or "or". (The parentheses are necessary because either|or matches "eitherr" or "eitheor".)
- The shorthand notation [a-z] means "all the characters in a range", and is easier to write and read than a|b|c|...|y|z.
- The characters ^ and $ are called anchors: they match the beginning and end of the line without matching any actual characters.
- If we want to put a special character like ., *, +, or | in a regular expression, we have to **escape** it with a backslash \. This means that /stop\./ only matches "stop.", while stop. matches "stops" as well.

Text	Pattern	Match	Explanation
abc	/b/	yes	character matches itself
	/b*/	yes	matches zero or more b's
	/z*/	yes	text contains zero z's, so pattern matches
	/z+/	no	text does not contain one or more z's
	/a.c/	yes	'.' matches the 'b'
	/^b/	no	text does not start with 'b'
abc123	/[a-z]+/	yes	contains one or more consecutive lower-case letters
	/^[a-z]+$/	no	digits in string prevent a match
	/^[a-z0-9]+$/	yes	whole string is lower-letters or digits
Dr. Toby	/(Dr|Prof)\./	yes	contains either "Dr" or "Prof" followed by literal '.'

Table H.1: Regular Expression Matches

This is a lot to digest, so Table H.1 shows a few examples. Regular expressions can match an intimidating number of other patterns, but are fairly easy to use in programs. Like strings and arrays, they are objects with methods: if `pattern` is a regular expression, then `string.test(pattern)` returns `true` if the pattern matches the string and `false` if it does not, while `string.match(pattern)` returns an array of matching substrings. If we add the modifier "g" after the closing slash of the regular expression to make it "global", then `string.match(pattern)` returns *all* of the matching substrings:

```
Tests = [
  'Jamie: james@geneinfo.org',
  'Zara: zetsure@bio123.edu',
  'Hong and Andrzej: hchui@euphoric.edu and aszego@euphoric.edu'
]

const pattern = /[a-z]+@[a-z]+\.[a-z]+/g

console.log(`pattern is ${pattern}`)
for (let test of Tests) {
  console.log(`tested against ${test}`)
  const matches = test.match(pattern)
  if (matches === null) {
    console.log('-no matches-')
  }
  else {
    for (let m of matches) {
      console.log(m)
    }
  }
}
```

```
pattern is /[a-z]+@[a-z]+\.[a-z]+/g

tested against Jamie: james@geneinfo.org
james@geneinfo.org

tested against Zara: zetsure@bio123.edu
-no matches-

tested against Hong and Andrzej: hchui@euphoric.edu and aszego@euphoric.edu
hchui@euphoric.edu
aszego@euphoric.edu
```

As powerful as they are, there are things that regular expressions can't do[1]. When it comes to pulling information out of text, though, they are easier to use and more efficient than long chains of substring tests. They can also be used to replace substrings and to split strings into pieces: please see the documentation[2] for more information.

---

[1] https://stackoverflow.com/questions/1732348/regex-match-open-tags-except-xhtml-self-contained-tags/1732454#1732454

[2] https://developer.mozilla.org/en-US/docs/Web/JavaScript/Guide/Regular_Expressions

Logging

The `console.log` function we have been using is a simple form of **logging**. We can use a library called Winston[1] to get more control and structure. By control, we mean that we can define levels for messages and a threshold for the logger, and only log things that are at least that important. This is much better than commenting and uncommenting messages, both because it involves less typing and because we can leave the logging code in place when we put our application into production to debug the problems that inevitably arise after we thought we were done. The standard error levels provided by Winston (and similar logging libraries) are `'error'`, `'warn'`, `'info'`, `'verbose'`, and `'debug'`, so if we set the threshold to `'info'`, then `'verbose'` and `'debug'` messages won't be displayed.

As for structure, Winston produces log messages as JSON objects by default so that other programs can easily read them. We can also configure it to produce CSV, or even define some custom format, though doing that will make everyone's life more difficult.

Whatever format we choose, we have to create and add a **transport** to tell Winston where messages should go. We will use one called `Console` that sends messages to the screen; we can also send messages to files, to remote logging servers, and so on. Note that we do *not* create a variable called `console` for the transport, because that will overwrite the `console` we have been using up until now, and yes, that took a couple of minutes to figure out...

```
const express = require('express')
const path = require('path')
const fs = require('fs')
const winston = require('winston')

const PORT = 3418
const root = process.argv[2]
const level = process.argv[3]

const transport = new winston.transports.Console()
winston.add(transport)
winston.level = level

// Main server object.
const app = express()

// Handle all requests.
app.use((req, res, next) => {
  const actual = path.join(root, req.url)
  fs.stat(actual, (err, stats) => {
    if (err) {
```

---

[1] https://github.com/winstonjs/winston

```
      winston.error(`Unable to find "${actual}"`)
      res.status(404).send(
        `<html><body><p>cannot read ${actual}</p></body></html>`)
    } else if (!stats.isFile()) {
      winston.error(`"${actual}" is not a file`)
      res.status(404).send(
        `<html><body><p>cannot read ${actual}</p></body></html>`)
    } else {
      winston.debug(`Serving "${actual}"`)
      fs.readFile(actual, 'utf-8', (err, data) => {
        res.status(200).send(data)
      })
    }
  })
})

app.listen(PORT, () => {
  winston.info(`Running on port ${PORT} with root ${root}`)
})
```

In the script above, we set the logging level with an extra command-line parameter. If we run the script with the `'debug'` level, all messages appear. If we run it with the `'info'` level, the startup message and the 404 error messages appear, and if we run it with the level `'error'` only the latter appear.

```
$ node src/logging/logging-server.js src/logging/web-dir/ info
```

```
{"message":"Running on port 3418 with root src/logging/web-dir/",
 "level":"info"}
{"message":"Unable to find \"src/logging/web-dir/missing.html\"",
 "level":"error"}
```

J Extensible Servers

Suppose we want to extend the server from Chapter 12 in some way. We could edit the source file and add some more URL handlers, or we could have it load JavaScript dynamically and run that.

```
const express = require('express')

const PORT = 3418

// Main server object.
const app = express()

// Handle all requests.
app.use((req, res, next) => {
  if (req.url.endsWith('.js')) {
    const libName = './'.concat(req.url.slice(0, -3))
    const dynamic = require(libName)
    const data = dynamic.page()
    res.status(200).send(data)
  }

  else {
    res.status(404).send(
      `<html><body><p>"${req.url}" not found</p></body></html>`)
  }
})

app.listen(PORT, () => { console.log(`listening on port ${PORT}...`) })
```

This simple server checks whether the path specified in the URL ends with `.js`. If so, it constructs something that looks like the name of a library by stripping off the `.js` and prefixing the stem with `./`, then uses `require` to load that file. Assuming the load is successful, it then calls the `page` function defined in that file. We can create a very simple plugin like this:

```
function page() {
  return ('<html><body><h1>Plugin Content</h1></body></html>');
}

module.exports = {
  page: page
}
```

If we run the server:

```
$ node src/extensible/dynamic.js
```

and then go to `http://localhost:4000/plugin.js`, we get back a page containing the title "Plugin Content".

This is an example of a very powerful technique. Rather than building everything into one program, we can provide a set of rules that plugins must follow so that people can add new functionality without rewriting what's already there. Each plugin must have an **entry point** like the function page so that the framework knows where to start.

K Using a Database

Our data manager (Chapter 11) got information from a single CSV file. That's fine for testing purposes, but real applications almost always use a database of some kind. There are many options these days for what kind, but **relational databases** continue to be the workhorses of the web.

Relational databases are manipulated using a language called **SQL**, which originally stood for "Structured Query Language" and is pronounced "sequel" or "ess cue ell" depending on whether the speaker is left or right handed. (Alternatives are collectively known as **NoSQL databases**, and use many different storage models.) We will use a SQL database because it's still the most common choice, but we won't try to introduce SQL itself: for that, see this short tutorial[1].

As an example problem, we will store information about workshops. Our database begins with a single **table** with three **fields** and two **records**:

```
drop table if exists Workshop;

create table Workshop(
    ident           integer unique not null primary key,
    name            text unique not null,
    duration        integer not null -- duration in minutes
);

insert into Workshop values(1, "Building Community", 60);
insert into Workshop values(2, "ENIAC Programming", 150);
```

In the rest of this tutorial, we will build a class to handle our interactions with a SQLite database, test it, and then put a web service on top of it.

K.1 STARTING POINT

Our class, imaginatively named `Database`, takes the path to the SQLite database file as a constructor parameter and creates a **connection manager** through which we can send queries and get results. We will create one method for each query we want to run, and one helper method to display query results. We will give all of the query methods the same **signature** so that can be handled interchangeably. The whole thing looks like this:

```
const sqlite3 = require('sqlite3')

class Database {

  constructor (path) {
```

---

[1] https://swcarpentry.github.io/sql-novice-survey/

```javascript
    this.db = new sqlite3.Database(path, sqlite3.OPEN_READWRITE, (err) => {
      if (err) this.fail(`Database open error ${err} for "${path}"`)
    })
  }

  getAll (args) {
    this.db.all(Q_WORKSHOP_GET_ALL, [], (err, rows) => {
      if (err) this.fail(err)
      this.display(rows)
    })
  }

  getOne (args) {
    this.db.all(Q_WORKSHOP_GET_ONE, args, (err, rows) => {
      if (err) this.fail(err)
      this.display(rows)
    })
  }

  display (rows) {
    for (let r of rows) {
      console.log(r)
    }
  }

  fail (msg) {
    console.log(msg)
    process.exit(1)
  }
}
```

This makes a lot more sense once we see what the queries look like:

```sql
const Q_WORKSHOP_GET_ALL = `
select
  Workshop.ident        as workshopId,
  Workshop.name         as workshopName,
  Workshop.duration     as workshopDuration
from
  Workshop
`
```

```sql
const Q_WORKSHOP_GET_ONE = `
select
  Workshop.ident        as workshopId,
  Workshop.name         as workshopName,
  Workshop.duration     as workshopDuration
from
  Workshop
where
  Workshop.ident = ?
`
```

It's easy to overlook, but the query to get details of one workshop has a question mark ? as the value of Workshop.ident. This means that the query expects us to

provide a parameter when we call it that will be substituted in for the question mark
to specify which workshop we're interested in. This is why the arguments passed to
getOne as args are then passed through to db.all; it's also why getAll takes an
args parameter, but ignores it and always passed [] (no extra values) to db.all
when running the query.

All right: what does the **driver** look like?

```
function main () {
  const path = process.argv[2]
  const action = process.argv[3]
  const args = process.argv.splice(4)
  const database = new Database(path)
  database[action](args)
}

main()
```

This is simple enough: it gets the path to the database file, the desired action, and any extra arguments from process.argv, then creates an instance of
the Database class and—um. And then it calls database[action](args), which
takes a moment to figure out. What's going on here is that an instance of a class
is just a special kind of object, and we can always look up an object's fields by
name using object[name], so if the string action (taken from the command-
line argument) is getAll or getOne, then database[action](args) is either
database.getAll(args) or database.getOne(args). This is clever, but if we
ask for an action like show or help or GetOne (with an upper-case 'G') then
database[action] doesn't exist and we get a very confusing error message. We
really should try to do better...

But before then, let's try running this:

```
$ node database-initial.js fixture.db getAll

{ workshopId: 1,
  workshopName: 'Building Community',
  workshopDuration: 60 }
{ workshopId: 2,
  workshopName: 'ENIAC Programming',
  workshopDuration: 150 }
```

That seems to have worked: getAll was called, and the result is an array of objects,
one per record, whose names are derived in an obvious way from the names of the
columns.

K.2 IN-MEMORY DATABASE

The previous example always manipulates database on disk. For testing purposes,
it's faster and safer to use an **in-memory database**. Let's modify the constructor of
Database to set this up:

```
  constructor (mode, path) {
    this.path = path
    switch (mode) {
    case 'memory' :
      const setup = fs.readFileSync(this.path, 'utf-8')
      this.db = new sqlite3.Database(':memory:', sqlite3.OPEN_READWRITE,
        (err) => {
          if (err) {
            this.fail(`In-memory database open error "${err}"`)
          }
      })
      this.db.exec(setup,(err) => {
        if (err) {
          this.fail(`Cannot initialize in-memory database from "${this.path}"`)
        }
      })
      break

    case 'file' :
      this.db = new sqlite3.Database(this.path, sqlite3.OPEN_READWRITE,
        (err) => {
          if (err) {
            this.fail(`Database open error ${err} for "${path}"`)
          }
      })
      break

    default :
      this.fail(`Unknown mode "${mode}"`)
      break
    }
  }
```

If the mode parameter is the string "memory", we create an in-memory database and initialize it by executing a file full of setup commands specified by the user—in our case, exactly the commands we showed at the start of the lesson. If the mode is "file", we interpret the file argument as the name of an on-disk database and proceed as before.

We put our error messages in ALL CAPS because that's the most annoying option easily available to us. Less annoyingly, we can use destructuring to handle command-line arguments in the driver:

```
function main () {
  const [mode, path, action, ...args] = process.argv.splice(2)
  const database = new Database(mode, path)
  database[action](args)
}
```

Here, the expression ...args means "take anything left over after the fixed names have been matched and put it in an array called args". With these changes in place, we can run a query to get details of the second workshop like this:

```
$ node database-mode.js memory fixture.sql getOne 2
```

```
{ workshopId: 2,
  workshopName: 'ENIAC Programming',
  workshopDuration: 150 }
```

After a bit of experimentation, we decide to take this even further to make testing easier. We will allow the driver to read the SQL script itself and pass that into
Database so that we can do the file I/O once and then repeatedly build a database
in memory for testing. That way, each of our tests will start with the database in
a known, predictable state, regardless of what other tests may have run before and
what changes they might have made to the database. Here are the changes to the
constructor:

```
constructor (mode, arg) {
  switch (mode) {
    case 'direct' :
      this._inMemory(arg)
      break

    case 'memory' :
      const setup = fs.readFileSync(arg, 'utf-8')
      this._inMemory(setup)
      break

    case 'file' :
      this._inFile(arg)
      break

    default :
      this.fail(`Unknown mode "${mode}"`)
      break
  }
}
```

And here are the supporting methods:

```
_inMemory (script) {
  this.db = new sqlite3.Database(':memory:', sqlite3.OPEN_READWRITE,
    (err) => {
      if (err) {
        this.fail(`In-memory database open error "${err}"`)
      }
  })
  this.db.exec(script,
    (err) => {
      if (err) {
        this.fail(`Unable to initialize in-memory database from "${script}"`)
      }
  })
}

_inFile (path) {
  this.db = new sqlite3.Database(path, sqlite3.OPEN_READWRITE, (err) => {
    if (err) this.fail(`Database open error "${err}" for "${path}"`)
  })
}
```

We also need to change the driver (and check, finally, that the requested action is
actually supported):

```
function main () {
  let [mode, setup, action, ...args] = process.argv.splice(2)
  if (mode === 'direct') {
    setup = fs.readFileSync(setup, 'utf-8')
  }
  const database = new Database(mode, setup)
  if (!(action in database)) {
    database.fail(`No such operation "${action}"`)
  }
  database[action](args)
}
```

K.3 MAKING IT TESTABLE

We put the database class and its driver in separate files so that applications can load
just the former. We will now change the database query methods to return results
for display rather than displaying them directly, since we will eventually want to
compare them or return them to a server rather than printing them:

```
class Database {

  // ...as before...

  getAll (args) {
    this.db.all(Q_WORKSHOP_GET_ALL, [], (err, rows) => {
      if (err) this.fail(err)
      return rows
    })
  }

  // ...as before...
}
```

The driver then looks like this:

```
const Database = require('./separate-database')

const display = (rows) => {
  for (let r of rows) {
    console.log(r)
  }
}

const main = () => {
  let [mode, path, action, ...args] = process.argv.splice(2)
  const db = new Database(mode, path)
  if (!(action in db)) {
    db.fail(`No such operation "${action}"`)
  }
  const result = db[action](args)
```

```
  display(result)
}

main()
```

Let's try running it:

```
$ node separate-driver.js file fixture.db getAll
```

```
  for (let r of rows) {
              ^

TypeError: Cannot read property 'Symbol(Symbol.iterator)' of undefined
    at display (/project/src/db/separate-driver.js:4:15)
    at main (/project/src/db/separate-driver.js:16:3)
```

Whoops: the run method of the database delivers results to a callback; its own result is therefore undefined, so there's nothing in the caller to print. The solution is to give the get methods a callback of their own:

```
class Database {

  // ...as before...

  getAll (args, callback) {
    this.db.all(Q_WORKSHOP_GET_ALL, [], (err, rows) => {
      if (err) this.fail(err)
      callback(rows)
    })
  }

  // ...as before...
}
```

We then change the driver to pass display to the database method it's calling:

```
const Database = require('./callback-database')

const display = (rows) => {
  for (let r of rows) {
    console.log(r)
  }
}

const main = () => {
  let [mode, path, action, ...args] = process.argv.splice(2)
  const db = new Database(mode, path)
  if (!(action in db)) {
    db.fail(`No such operation "${action}"`)
  }
  db[action](args, display)
}

main()
```

This looks strange the first few (dozen) times, but it's the way JavaScript works: instead of asking for something and then operating on it, we say, "Here's what we want to do once results are available."

K.4   TESTING

We can finally write some tests:

```
const assert = require('assert')
const Database = require('./callback-database')

const FIXTURE = `
drop table if exists Workshop;

create table Workshop(
  ident          integer unique not null primary key,
  name           text unique not null,
  duration       integer not null -- duration in minutes
);

insert into Workshop values(1, "Building Community", 60);
insert into Workshop values(2, "ENIAC Programming", 150);
`

describe('database', () => {

  it('should return all workshops', (done) => {
    expected = [
      { workshopName: 'Building Community',
        workshopDuration: 60, workshopId: 1 },
      { workshopName: 'ENIAC Programming',
        workshopDuration: 150, workshopId: 2 }
    ]
    new Database('direct', FIXTURE).getAll([], (results) => {
      assert.deepEqual(results, expected,
                       'Got expected workshops')
      done()
    })
  })

  it('should return one workshop', (done) => {
    expected = [
      { workshopName: 'Building Community',
        workshopDuration: 60, workshopId: 1 }
    ]
    new Database('direct', FIXTURE).getOne(1, (results) => {
      assert.deepEqual(results, expected,
                       'Got single expected workshop')
      done()
    })
  })

  it('can only get workshops that exist', (done) => {
    new Database('direct', FIXTURE).getOne(99, (results) => {
      assert.deepEqual(results, [],
```

```
                          'Got no workshops matching nonexistent key')
      done()
    })
  })

})
```

Each test has the same structure: we define the expected result, create an entirely new database in memory, and then call the method being tested, passing it the fixture and the callback that will receive results. That callback uses `assert` to check results and done to signal that the test has completed.

K.5   UPDATING THE DATABASE

The data manager we built in Chapter 11 only let us read data; we couldn't modify it. Let's add a bit more to our database class to support **mutation**:

```
// ...imports as before...

const Q_WORKSHOP_GET_ALL = // ...as before...
const Q_WORKSHOP_GET_ONE = // ...as before...

const Q_WORKSHOP_ADD = `
insert into Workshop(name, duration) values(?, ?);
`

const Q_WORKSHOP_DELETE = `
delete from Workshop where ident = ?;
`

class Database {

  constructor (mode, arg) {
    // ...as before...
  }
  getAll (args, callback) {
    // ...as before...
  }
  getOne (args, callback) {
    // ...as before...
  }

  addOne (args, callback) {
    this.db.run(Q_WORKSHOP_ADD, args, function (err, rows) {
      if (err) this.fail(err)
      callback([], this.lastID)
    })
  }

  deleteOne (args, callback) {
    this.db.run(Q_WORKSHOP_DELETE, args, (err, rows) => {
      if (err) this.fail(err)
      callback([], undefined)
    })
```

```
  }

  fail (msg) {
    // ...as before...
  }
  _inMemory (script) {
    // ...as before...
  }
  _inFile (path) {
    // ...as before...
  }
}

module.exports = Database
```

The additions are straightforward: the query that does the work is passed to
this.db.run along with the incoming arguments that specify what is to be added
or deleted, and an empty list of rows is passed to the action callback (since adding
and deleting don't return anything). Testing involves a little more typing, since we
want to check that the database is in the right state after the operation:

```
// ...imports as before...

const FIXTURE = // ...as before...

describe('mutating database', () => {

  it('can add a workshop', (done) => {
    const duration = 35, name = 'Creating Bugs'
    const db = new Database('direct', FIXTURE)
    db.addOne([name, duration], function (results, lastID) {
      assert.deepEqual(results, [], 'Got empty list as result when adding')
      assert.equal(lastID, 3, 'Got the correct last ID after adding')
      db.getAll([], (results) => {
        expected = [
          { workshopName: 'Building Community',
            workshopDuration: 60, workshopId: 1 },
          { workshopName: 'ENIAC Programming',
            workshopDuration: 150, workshopId: 2 },
          { workshopName: name,
            workshopDuration: duration, workshopId: 3 }
        ]
        assert.deepEqual(results, expected,
                         'Got expected workshops after add')
        done()
      })
    })
  })

  it('can delete a workshop', (done) => {
    const db = new Database('direct', FIXTURE)
    db.deleteOne([1], (results, lastID) => {
      assert.equal(lastID, undefined, 'Expected last ID to be undefined')
      assert.deepEqual(results, [], 'Got empty list as result when deleting')
      db.getAll([], (results) => {
```

```
        expected = [
          { workshopName: 'ENIAC Programming',
            workshopDuration: 150, workshopId: 2 }
        ]
        assert.deepEqual(results, expected,
                       'Got expected workshops after delete')
        done()
      })
    })
  })
})
```

K.6   EXERCISES

COPYING RECORDS

Write a program that copies all the rows from the table Workshop in a database source.db to a table with the same name in a new database backup.db.

FILTERING RECORDS

Add a new method to the Database class to get all workshops that are longer than a specified time:

```
const db = new Database(path)
const rows = db.getLongerThan(100)
assert.deepEqual(rows, [
  {workshopName: 'ENIAC Programming', workshopDuration: 150, workshopId: 2}
])
```

Your Database.getLongerThan method's SQL query will need to use a where clause that selects specific records.

MORE FILTERING

The SQL query encapsulated in the variable below can be used to find all workshops whose duration falls within a range.

```
const Q_WORKSHOP_DURATION_RANGE = `
select
  Workshop.ident        as workshopId,
  Workshop.name         as workshopName,
  Workshop.duration     as workshopDuration
from
  Workshop
where
  (Workshop.duration <= ?) and (Workshop.duration >= ?)
`
```

What do the ?s mean in this query? Write another method for the Database class called getWithinLengthRange([args]) that uses this query, taking arguments from the commandline as before. What happens when you provide the wrong number of arguments to this function? Or if you provide them in the wrong order? Can you write a test that provides more useful feedback than this?

HANDLING ERRORS

The `Database` class prints a message and exits when it detects an error. This is bad practice, and I should be ashamed of having done it. The right thing to do is to **throw** an **exception** that the main program can **catch** and handle however it wants.

1. Modify the code to do this.
2. Modify the tests to check that the right exceptions are thrown when they should be.

USING A DATABASE WITH A SERVER

Rewrite the capstone project in Chapter 15 to use a database instead of a file for data storage.

L ∣ Deploying

Running applications on our laptop is fine for testing, but sooner or later we will want to put them on the web for others to use. A general discussion of **deployment** is outside the scope of these lessons, particularly because it shouldn't be done without thinking carefully about security, but there are now a few entry-level platforms you can try out.

One of the simplest of these platforms is Glitch[1], which is designed to help students build their first interactive websites. It isn't designed to host large, high-traffic applications, but is great for prototyping and classroom use. To try it out, go to https://glitch.com and create a free account. You can then click on the "New Project" button in the upper right and select `hello-express`, which will create a basic Express application. This project contains a handful of files that you should find familiar:

- `README.md`: a description of the project formatted in Markdown.
- `package.json`: the NPM package listing for the project.
- `server.js`: the server. This is initially set up to route requests for / to `/views/index.html`, but can be made as complicated as we want. Note that it uses a variable called `__dirname` (with two leading underscores) to get the name of the directory that the server is running in; this is needed because Glitch controls where our application runs.
- `views/index.html`: the application's home page. We can add as many other pages as we want, but they have to go in the `views` folder.
- `public/client.js`: the user interface code that is run in the browser. The `public` folder acts as the root directory for the server, so inside `views/index.html` and other web pages, we refer to `public/client.js` simply as `/client.js`.
- `public/style.css`: the CSS that styles the application. Again, inside `views/index.html` we refer to this file as `/style.css` without naming the `public` folder.
- `.env`: a shell script that defines any secret configuration variables the application needs, such as passwords for databases. Unlike the files above, this one *isn't* automatically copied when someone clones our application. If we define a variable called `PASSWORD` in this file, then our server can get its value (as a string) using `process.env.PASSWORD`. Life might have been a little simpler if Glitch's creators had used a JSON file instead of a shell script, but as long as we stick to simple `NAME=VALUE` pairs, we'll be OK.

---

[1] https://glitch.com/

Figure L.1: Glitch Deployment

Two things that *aren't* automatically present are a license and a Code of Conduct, but both can easily be added by clicking on the "New File" button. Several widely-used open source licenses are available, and the Code of Conduct is based on one that is also widely used in open source projects. Adding both makes it clear what we are allowing and expecting people to do with our project.

The "Rewind" button in the bottom of the file explorer lets us view the project's history. Glitch uses Git to store changes, but presents those changes as a timeline so that we can scroll backward and forward to see what was altered when. The "Tools" button (also in the bottom of the file explorer) gives us access to run logs and performance information, and lets us connect our project to a repository on GitHub.

Behind the scenes, every Glitch application runs in a virtual machine. Any data that it creates or modifies (such as files on disk or SQLite databases Appendix K) are automatically saved, up to a limit of 128 MByte. An application is allowed to handle several thousand requests per hour; if it doesn't receive any requests for 5 minutes, the virtual machine is put to sleep. It is automatically restarted the next time a request comes in, but there will be a lag as it wakes up.

Index